HOW GOD TREATS HIS FRIENDS

HOW GOD TREATS HIS FRIENDS

ROBERT FYALL

CHRISTIAN FOCUS PUBLICATIONS

© 1995 Robert Fyall
ISBN 1-85792-115-1

Published by
Christian Focus Publications Ltd
Geanies House, Fearn, Ross-shire,
IV20 1TW, Scotland, Great Britain.

Printed and bound in Great Britain by
Cox & Wyman Ltd, Reading, Berkshire

Cover design by Donna Macleod

Contents

Foreword

I have sometimes thought that it is one of the great 'treats' of life in the Christian church to have friends who combine special expertise in the study of the Old Testament with a commitment to share its riches. To read, or to listen to exposition which is sensitive to its literature, language, imagery and themes is a high privilege. It is to have the mind stretched to take in the sheer greatness of the covenant-making God, to have the will redirected to serve him, and, yes, to have the emotions cleansed. Those – like Robert Fyall – who are able to handle the Old Testament with such skill are among the treasures of the church.

Dr Fyall is an Old Testament scholar who currently teaches at St John's College, Durham and brings to his writing his considerable scholarly expertise. But more than that, in these pages he places his gifts at the disposal of non-experts like ourselves, and invites us to read through the Book of Job with him, as friends. As we do so, we will soon feel that he is sitting beside us and – as a patient teacher – is pointing out many of the things he knows we need to learn, and asking us, 'Do you see this? And this? And this?' One indication of Robert Fyall's gifts is that when *he* points things out to you, they become hard to miss!

I think I can promise you that the experience of reading *How God Treats His Friends* will be very rewarding indeed. In his easy and pleasant style Dr Fyall will show you wisdom, insight, pathos, challenge and encouragement – and all from one priceless book of the Bible.

The Book of Job is a majestic piece of literature by any standard. But it is more; it is God's word, and with the help of these chapters you will at times be stunned by its power and find it speaking to you in a multitude of fresh ways.

How God Treats His Friends has many fine points. Perhaps the most important of them is that its interpretation of the Book of Job is consistent and convincing. It would be wrong to steal a book's thunder, but perhaps it will whet your appetite to know that, unlike many commentaries and studies of Job, Dr Fyall's exposition persuasively interprets it from beginning to end. Those who have read other works on Job may well find themselves saying as they come to the conclusion of this one, '*Now* it is clear what the Book of Job is about; it all makes sense; why didn't I see that before?'.

A further strength should be mentioned. As someone whose interests lie in the world of the ancient Near East in which the Old Testament is set, Dr Fyall is sensitive to the ideas, beliefs and concepts which were part of that paganly religious environment. He shows how the Book of Job, like other biblical books, used the language and concepts of its day in the service of divine revelation. To some readers of the Old Testament this may be a new and strange concept to grasp. But in many ways it will underline the sheer power with which 'In the past God spoke to our forefathers' (Hebrews 1:1). The marvellous thing is that Robert Fyall deals with all this in a way that demonstrates how Scripture speaks to our own time, and indeed to our own needs too.

These qualities alone would make *How God Treats His Friends* a must-buy. Careful biblical interpretation at its best is worth reading for its own sake. But add to this pearls of wisdom (dropped, it seems, almost in passing) which help us to study the Bible better for ourselves, as well as insights which will help us to live the Christian life more consistently – and here you have a book of great value.

'No-one who reads the Book of Job can remain indifferent; it is an exhilarating if often bruising experience', writes Dr Fyall. So, prepare to be bruised and exhilarated as you turn these pages with your Bible beside you. As you read you will come to appreciate the Book of Job in a new way; you will also want to read the Old Testament much more. And I suspect you will be on the look-out for another book from the same author. But until then, *How God Treats His Friends* will be worth re-reading!

Sinclair B Ferguson
Westminster Theological Seminary, Philadelphia

Introduction

This book began life as a series of talks on Job given to Durham Christian Union in January and February 1992. The interest and enthusiasm shown by the students encouraged me to believe that the material might be of interest to a wider public. I am most grateful to the staff at Christian Focus, especially Mr. Malcolm Maclean, Managing Editor, for their acceptance of this project and their care and diligence as tapes were translated into a readable script. I am also grateful to Dr Sinclair B Ferguson of Westminster Theological Seminary, Philadelphia, for providing the foreword.

This is not an academic book, but much of the basic study was done in preparation for my doctoral thesis on Job for Edinburgh University. Those readers familiar with the vast literature of commentaries, studies and articles on Job will see at many points that I have taken particular views on disputed issues. The main aim of this book, however, is to help people to read and begin to appreciate some of the treasures of one of the profoundest books in the Bible and to see how it applies to the world's needs and our lives as we near the end of the century.

I am happy to be able to thank a number of people without whom this book could not have

been written. Professor John Gibson, recently re-
tired from Edinburgh University, fired me with
enthusiasm for Job during my theological studies in
Edinburgh and later supervised my thesis. My debt
to him is very great. Over the last five years I have
explored Job with students at St John's College,
Durham and for the many stimulating discussions
and shared insights I am most grateful. Marianne
Young of the secretarial staff of St John's College
typed the manuscript and did so with cheerful
efficiency.

My children, Carmen and Drummond, helped to
keep my feet on the ground. But above all, my wife
Thelma gave the loving support and patient encouragement which was the context in which the book
was written.

It was in my father and mother's home that I first
learned to love the Bible and I want to dedicate this
book to my mother and the memory of my father.

Bob Fyall
1995

The Structure of the Book of Job

The book falls into a number of fairly clearly defined parts and it would be useful to have a good idea of the way drama/argument develops.

1. Prologue (Chs. 1 and 2)
  1st Test (Family and Possession)
  2nd Test (Health and Sanity)

2. Poetic Dialogue (Chs. 3-41)
This can be further subdivided:
  a. *Introduction* (Ch. 3) - main themes of death and loss of meaning suggested.

  b. *1st Speech Cycle* (Chs. 4-14):
  Eliphaz (Chs. 4-5) - Defence of traditional Wisdom teaching.

  Job's 1st reply (Chs. 6-7) - Both God and his friends have rejected him.

  Bildad (Ch. 8) - God creates and governs justly.

  Job's 2nd reply (Chs. 9-10) - Legal disputation with God.

  Zophar (Ch. 11) - God is unerringly just.

Job's 3rd reply (Chs. 12-14) - Frailty and transience of humans and apparent arbitrariness of God.

c. *2nd Speech Cycle* (Chs. 15-21):
Eliphaz (15) - Questions Job's wisdom and innocence.

Job's 4th Reply (Chs. 16-17) - Enmity and hostility of God.

Bildad (Ch. 18) - Fate of the wicked (i.e. Job).

Job's 5th Reply (Ch. 19) - Challenge to God to clear his name.

Zophar (Ch. 20) - Retribution comes to the wicked (i.e. Job).

Job's 6th Reply (Ch. 21) - Fate does not always correspond to virtue.

d. *3rd Speech Cycle* (Chs. 22-27):
Eliphaz (Ch. 22) - God must be punishing Job for his sins.

Job's 7th Reply (Chs. 23-24) - Why does God allow injustice?

Bildad (Ch. 25) - sour tirade on God's power.

Job's 8th Reply (Chs. 26-27) - Mysteries of God's power and providence.

e. *The Wisdom Poem* (Ch. 28):
Interlude to evoke Divine Wisdom.

f. *Job's Apologia* (Chs. 29-31):
Final statement of his integrity.

g. *Elihu* (Chs. 32-37):
Speculation on place of suffering.

h. *Yahweh's Speeches* (Chs. 38-42):
1st Speech (Ch. 38-39): Marvels of inanimate and animate creation.

2nd Speech (Ch. 40-41): Behemoth and Leviathan: images of evil.

3. Epilogue (Ch. 42):
Job restored and blessed.

1

IS GOD THE AUTHOR OF EVIL?
(Job 1, 2)

St. Teresa of Avila once went through a very long period of depression and darkness towards the end of which she had a vision of God. God said to her, 'This is how I always treat my friends.' 'Then Lord,' she replied, 'it is not surprising that you have so few.'

That grim jest is very much in the spirit of the book of Job and indeed of much of the Old Testament. Over and over again we find a seemingly irreverent questioning of God and of his purposes. The Psalms are full of expressions such as 'How long, oh Lord?' The book of Jeremiah contains some of the most bitter questioning of God in or out of the Bible. The most striking of these is in 20:7: 'LORD, you deceived me', where the word used is actually the Hebrew word for 'seduced'. This questioning of God is indeed characteristic of Jewish literature surfacing, for example, on a lighter level in *The Fiddler on the Roof* : 'Would it interrupt some vast eternal plan, if I were a wealthy man?'

But nowhere is this questioning more anguished or sustained than in the book of Job. The book is provocative and mind-bending. Many familiar certainties dissolve and, like a rider on a roller-coaster, the reader wonders if the ground will ever be safely reached.

Job belongs to what is often called Wisdom Literature, along with Proverbs, Ecclesiastes and other parts of the Bible such as some of the Psalms (e.g. 1, 49, 73) and the Song of Songs. The term 'Wisdom' is a wider concept in Biblical literature than the English term suggests. Wisdom includes what we would call expertise, skill, good advice and the like. Thus in Exodus 31:3 Bezaleel, the maker of the Tent in the desert, is described as 'wise'; in Isaiah 40:20 and Jeremiah 10:9 craftsmen are so described and in Ezekiel 27:8,9 the term is applied to shipwrights. At the court of David it was used of political advisors such as Ahithopel and Hushai. The term thus has implications not only of intellectual understanding but of grasping the right way to live. Wisdom is the art of living well in harmony with the principles on which God has made the universe.

True wisdom belongs to God alone: 'To God belong wisdom and power' (Job 12:13). That wisdom is at the heart of creation: 'How many are your works, O LORD, in wisdom you made them all' (Psalm 104:24). It is the foundation of right living: 'The fear of the LORD is the beginning of wisdom' (Proverbs 1:7). Yet the paradox of the book of Job is this: Job exemplifies wisdom, he has all the qualities the Bible commends and yet he is plunged into deep and black tragedy.

The structure of the book is that chapters 1 and 2 are an apparently simple story, a kind of traditional-tale and that is reverted to in chapter 42. The bulk of the book, chapters 3-41, is a tremendous dramatic poem. An outline of the book can be found on pages 7-9 and it would be helpful to refer to that from time to time.

The situation of Job creates the occasion for a debate - if debate is the right word - on the problems of evil and suffering. There is on one level a straightforward issue: Is good rewarded and evil punished? In one sense that is what the book is about. But, on a deeper level, the question is: Can we trust, can we believe in, can we have confidence in the God who created the worlds? It is no accident that this question is explored in what is perhaps the greatest poetry in the Old Testament. Thus to respond to and appreciate the book, the reader must be sensitive to the imagery and metaphors, to the pictures and the whole dazzling cascade of ideas in the Old Testament's greatest literary work.

To call Job the greatest literary work in the Old Testament is to draw attention to the fact that its profound message is embodied in equally great literature. The vivid and colourful imagery expresses the ideas in memorable ways. The sense of the vastness and mystery of the universe is not merely stated, but visually captured in chapters such as 26 and 38. Moreover the artistry is not simply eloquence, but extends to the finest details, and the ideas are expressed with a delicacy and verve. No-one who reads the book can remain indifferent; it is an exhilarating if often bruising experience.

Chapters 1 and 2 raise in an acute form the question: Is God the author of evil? When dreadful things happen; when cancer strikes in the life of some young mother, who dies and leaves a husband and small children; when a tidal wave sweeps over and destroys an entire village; when war and violence tear apart communities; when appalling disasters come into our lives; is the blame for these to be laid on God's presumably broad shoulders? Is God the author of evil?

To help explore this question from chapters 1 and 2 it is useful to examine the three main characters in the story: Job, God and Satan. We shall look first at the individual who is the storm centre of these disasters; then at God himself who appears to be responsible; and finally at Satan who is the agent of Job's agonies.

Job

We begin, then, with Job himself. The writer cleverly builds up a picture which makes him an average human being rather than a privileged Israelite. He lives in the land of Uz, possibly somewhere in the Arabian desert. The setting sounds patriarchal but, unlike Abraham, Job is not given a family tree. The point of this is that Job is being presented as a representative of humanity as a whole, not specifically as an Israelite. Indeed it is characteristic of the Old Testament that many of the most important events of Israel's faith do not take place on Israelite soil. We may mention as examples the call of Moses, the giving of the law, and the stories of divine intervention in Ezekiel and Daniel. This underlines the fact that the message of the Old Testament is for humanity as a whole.

Now what kind of person is Job? It is significant that his character is mentioned before his wealth. He is 'blameless' (1:1), a word used of clean animals offered for sacrifice (e.g. Leviticus 22:18-20: 'you must present a male without defect from the cattle, sheep or goats'). He is also 'upright' (1:1), a word which suggests on the one hand that he is a person who is utterly honest and open, and on the other hand, a person who is generous and kind. He also 'feared God' and this is the quality which Proverbs 1:7 describes as 'the beginning of wisdom'.

In other words, Job is presented as someone who exemplifies all the qualities of wisdom. He was also a widely known figure, mentioned in Ezekiel 14:14 and 20 as a heroic figure from the past, along with Daniel and Noah. And he is held up for admiration in the letter of James: 'You have heard of Job's perseverance' (5:11). Now the point is not that he was sinless, not that he was perfect, but that he was genuinely good. Job is in no sense a hypocrite; his goodness is in no sense superficial, he is genuinely good, genuinely caring, genuinely compassionate. Even Satan argues that Job is genuinely good, although he has his own reasons for so arguing.

What we have in this story, then, is not suffering that comes as the result of mistakes or wrongdoing. We are all familiar with that. If I crash my car at 100 mph into a brick wall I will experience the consequences of my own stupidity, if I am still alive to experience them. If we tell lies and cheat, then eventually we will be caught out, and so on. What we are dealing with here is a genuinely good person who is overwhelmed by a series of appalling disasters.

This is emphasised by the fact that God calls Job 'my servant' (1:8). Now in the Old Testament, the title 'my servant' is not simply used of pious individuals, but rather of those who have a singularly close and deep relationship with God. More especially it is used of Moses and the prophets, those whose lives are devoted to God. What is happening to Job is a particularly devastating example of how God 'treats his friends'.

The mystery is compounded by the fact that disaster strikes immediately after Job offers sacrifices and prayers for his family. Hard on the heels of his prayers, a series of hammer blows robs him of his family, his possessions, his health and almost his sanity. The way the story is told (e.g. 1:16 - 'while he was still speaking another messenger came and said ...') underlines the relentlessness of the catastrophes. Then in 1:14, the domestic scene of oxen ploughing and donkeys grazing highlights the cruel nature of the events. Suspense grows as we wait for Job's reaction. How is this man going to react to these catastrophes?

His first reaction comes in 1:21: 'Naked I came from my mother's womb, and naked I shall depart. The LORD gave and the LORD has taken away; may the name of the LORD be praised.' God, asserts Job in the face of these catastrophes, is responsible for the whole of life.

His next reaction is: 'shall we accept good from God, and not trouble?' (2:10). Now the word 'accept' is not a particularly apt translation. What the Hebrew word suggests is 'shall we not actively cooperate with God in whatever he sends us?' This is a point of great importance. Job is not saying that terrible things have happened but we must grin and bear it. Rather he is saying that whatever happens we must continue to love God, trust him and keep on walking with him.

Thus the Job of chapters 1 and 2 is a person of enormous integrity, a person who is walking with God, and who fears God. In spite of this he is not only overwhelmed by a series of disasters, but is overwhelmed by them immediately after praying

that they would not happen. Many have had an
experience like that. They have prayed with ear-
nestness and with faith for something, believing
God would grant it, and then found themselves face
to face with the very situation against which they
prayed and which they believed God would never
allow to happen.

God

That brings us conveniently to the second main
point of this chapter, which is the part that God
plays. Is God the author of evil? Now the Old
Testament is not afraid in places to say just that.
Amos 3:6 says: 'When evil comes to a city, has not
the LORD caused it?' Even more striking is the stark
statement of Isaiah 45:7: 'I, the LORD, create good
and evil.' But the big question is: Does God create
evil in the same direct way that he creates good?
Does evil come from the hand of God in exactly the
same way that good comes from the hand of God?
Nor is this simply an Old Testament problem. John
1:3 reads, 'Through him all things were made;
without him nothing was made that has been made.'
That presumably includes all the bad things as well
as the good things.

What does the author of Job do in the face of this
problem? What he does is to show us that earthly
events happen as a result of decisions made in
heaven. This, however, does not imply a mechanical and deterministic universe. In other words, God

is not like a machine operator who presses a series of switches and buttons and the machine goes on in a totally predetermined manner. What the author presents is a far more dynamic picture, the picture of the heavenly court, the sons of God or the angels who present themselves before God.

The idea of the heavenly court or council is a very common one in the ancient world. Israel's Canaanite neighbours believed that the gods met in council on a mountain, and some Old Testament passages speak of the council or courts of God.

Psalm 82 speaks of God standing in the council of the gods to give judgment. Another significant passage is 1 Kings 22:8ff: Ahab, King of Israel, and Jehoshaphat, King of Judah, ask the Lord for advice about whether to go and take the Syrian city of Ramoth Gilead. A prophet called Micaiah tells of a vision of the heavenly court: 'I saw the LORD sitting on his throne with all the host of heaven standing round him on his right and on his left'; the Lord then sends a lying spirit to entice Ahab to go up to Ramoth Gilead to his death. In Isaiah 6 the prophet gives an account of his call, and in verse 8 of that chapter he hears the voice of the Lord speaking to his entourage: 'Whom shall I send? And who will go for us?' The presence of the heavenly court is implied by the plural *us*, and given tangible form by the presence of the seraphim.

These, and other passages, present this picture of the heavenly court where events on earth are orchestrated and where situations that emerge in this world have their origins.

Now this helps to suggest at least the beginnings of a solution to the basic problem of the book of Job which, put succinctly, is this: God is good, Job is innocent, and yet the calamities which come on Job come from the hand of God himself. The presence of the heavenly court establishes on the one hand the uniqueness of God and his responsibility for what happens, for the other members of the court exist only in relation to him and derive their authority from him. Yet on the other hand it emphasises the presence and activity of other powers in the universe. To put this another way: God is supreme, God is in control of what happens, but nevertheless there are other powers in the universe who influence events.

This is a dramatic way of showing that God's creation, God's providence, is not something mechanical, but something that involves a series of relationships, something that involves interaction between God and his creatures. This means that the answer to the question 'Is God the author of evil?' is not a simple 'yes' or 'no'. We shall continue to explore this basic question, not only in this chapter, but throughout the rest of the book.

That said, what are we to make of the fact that God actually incites Satan to move against Job? Satan comes into the heavenly court and God challenges him: 'Have you considered my servant

Job?' (1:8). God throws down the gauntlet, as it were, and says, 'In all your comings and goings on the earth, have you seen such an outstanding example of faithfulness and integrity?'

It is necessary to nail Satan's accusation: 'Does Job fear God for nothing?' because he is attacking not only Job's integrity but God's. This is seen when he goes on to say, 'Have you not put a hedge around him and his household and everything he has?' (1:10). The story as it unfolds will appear to challenge God's integrity just as much as Job's. Is Job's integrity simply a fair-weather faith? Does he simply believe God when his cupboard is full, when his family is flourishing, when his flocks and herds are expanding and all is well? That, of course, is the big practical question that faces us so often. Do we believe in God only when everything is going well for us? Is belief in God dependent on plenty of money, flourishing relationships, a good career and robust health?

But there is a further issue. God is not just placing Job on the line, God is placing his own integrity on the line as well. This is worth exploring a little. It is not enough to argue, as some have done, that since God knows what will happen, it is pointless to subject Job to these tests of faith. What Augustine pointed out long ago in relation to Abraham is equally true of Job, namely, that whatever God knew, Abraham certainly did not know that his faith was equal to the test. Likewise Job did not

know, when these calamities struck him, that he
would emerge at the other end with his faith intact.
Nor do the readers know this and hence the test is
real. God is not going through a charade for his own
amusement. Job's faith must be demonstrated to be
not a fair-weather faith. It must be proved to Satan
and indeed to the whole universe that Job does not
fear God simply because God has blessed him.

Satan

We now look at the third main actor in the drama:
Satan, or more accurately since the Hebrew text has
the definite article, 'the Satan'. The Satan is mentioned by that title twice elsewhere in the Old
Testament. He occurs in 1 Chronicles 21 where he
incites King David to number the people, and
thereby to place faith in armies and prestige rather
than in God. He is mentioned in Zechariah 3 where
he proceeds against Joshua the High Priest. The
word, probably as a common noun meaning the
'accuser', also occurs in some of the Psalms. Here,
however, in Job, the figure plays a more striking
role.

Now this story is anything but naive, and the
more we read Job 1 and 2, the more subtleties and
depths appear. God does indeed challenge Satan,
that is true, but notice how quickly Satan replies. It
is almost as if Satan had come to the heavenly court
with the specific object of proceeding against Job.

Another detail worth noting is the deliberate

word play on the phrases 'the Hand of God' and 'the Hand of Satan'. For example, see 1:10-12 and 2:5-6. Job is in God's hands and God allows him to be in Satan's hands. In many ways this is the key to what is happening throughout the book. A large part of the agony of Job is that he imagines God has turned hostile. Part of the problem of the book is that Job has this enemy in heaven who is trying to destroy him and very often Job confuses the enemy with God himself.

Now we can dodge the problem; we can say that while God gives permission he is not really responsible for what Satan does. The trouble is that in any society, in any kind of institution or body, the person ultimately responsible is the person who must carry the can for the activities of subordinates who are permitted to behave in a particular way. This, of course, has been one of the big problems of human history. Thus, for example, Nazi war criminals claimed at the end of the Second World War that they engaged in terrifying violence and genocide because they had been ordered to by higher authorities. The higher is ultimately responsible for the lower.

What is happening in the book is a titanic struggle between the forces of good and evil, between God and the Satan. Job has become the battleground for that struggle, a struggle which ultimately is to find its climax in the Cross, where another man does battle with this titanic enemy on

our behalf. Now the friends of Job fail to see this
about Job, they explain everything that is happening mechanically, and in chapter 3 we shall explore
this further. Plainly, however, if we miss this supernatural dimension, this titanic struggle between
God and his enemy, whose focus and battleground
is Job himself, then we will miss what the book is
really about.

Three observations are worth making. The first
is that God is in control and Satan can operate only
within the divine permission. In chapter 38 of Job,
God says to the waves of the sea, 'This far you may
come and no further', and that is exactly what he
says to Satan in chapter 1.

Now, depending on our faith at any given moment, the fact that God is in control may cause us to
thank him or to dread him. Probably all of us have
had the kind of experience where the problem is not
that we do not believe God to be in control, but that
we secretly do not trust God to work out a scenario
we will like. We do not doubt that God is in control,
nor even that he has our best interests at heart. What
we do doubt is that he knows as well as we do what
our best interests are.

It is wonderful to feel that God is in control when
things are going well, but when things go disas-
trously wrong, we sometimes feel, as C. S. Lewis
felt in *A Grief Observed,* that we are in the hands of
a 'cosmic sadist'. God seems hostile and the light
has gone out of the sky. This is particularly the

theme of Job 3 which we shall explore in the next chapter.

The second observation is that evil powers opposed to God are active in the universe. This is something which must be recognised and an area in which two extremes have to be avoided. We have to avoid the extreme of overdoing it. There are some Christians who want to find the devil everywhere. If you lose your temper, your need deliverance. If you have a headache, it is the result of demonic activity. That is not to pour scorn on divine healing but rather to point out that sometimes we see the activities of the devil and demons in situations which can be explained quite adequately by our own fallen nature. At the other extreme there are those who ridicule and reject any idea of demonic activity and attribute everything to natural temperament and circumstances.

Now it is important to avoid both these extremes. These powers are real, they are prominent, but they can act only within God's permission, and thus the big question we have to ask is: Where does Satan go after chapter 2? Why does he not appear in the book again?

My argument, to anticipate, is that he does appear in the book again, indeed he appears regularly in various guises, and finally that the tremendous picture of Leviathan in chapter 41 is in fact an embodiment of the evil one himself, 'the ancient prince of hell' of whom Luther speaks. And moreover, he so subtly imitates God that for most of the book Job imagines that the enemy who is attacking him is God himself. This is developed by Paul in 2 Corinthians where he speaks of the devil transforming himself into an angel of light (11:14). One of Satan's most dangerous devices is to speak with a voice that can be mistaken for God's own and act in a way that can be misunderstood as divine action.

The third observation is that all this is being experienced by a human being. It is not merely someone speculating on the mysteries of existence and the problem of evil. This is a human being sitting on an ash heap in harsh and bitter agony and loneliness. The book of Job is an enormously practical book. It is a facing up to the existence of dark, sinister cosmic forces which are opposed to God and to his gospel. To understand it, more than theology is needed, though we do need that; more than clear thinking is needed, although that is necessary as well. But above all courage, faith, and open and teachable spirits are needed as we explore this great book together.

WHERE IS GOD WHEN IT HURTS?
(Job 3)

With Job 3 we are plunged into an altogether more sinister world where dark, cosmic crosscurrents are flowing. This introduces us to a world which we will need to grapple with and of whose power we will need to be aware. This is more necessary because there is a kind of Christianity which advocates that our lives should always be filled with laughter and happiness, and our worship always filled with praise and light-heartedness; the kind of Christianity that would have had Jesus singing a chorus at the grave of Lazarus. Not that joy, exuberance and happiness are wrong; far from it, they are necessary parts of our worship and living.

Nevertheless, these do not cover the whole of life and especially they do not address the question raised starkly by Job 3: 'Where is God when it hurts?' There are times when it does hurt, and hurt badly. If you are suffering some kind of depression or the effect of some disaster, if you feel that God has abandoned you, what are you to do when confronted with this kind of hyped-up, triumphalist Christianity?

In this powerful and bleak poem Job eventually breaks the seven-day silence and expresses his feelings and his agony in a kind of soliloquy. The dialogue proper has not yet begun. Job has not yet begun to speak to his friends; they have not yet begun to reply.

There are two initial comments to be made. The first is this: the experience of depression and suffering does not mean that God is angry with us. The Bible, the New Testament as well as the Old Testament, shows that those who walk most closely with God are often those who go through the deepest and darkest depressions. The book of Jeremiah, for example, has a passage almost identical to part of this chapter, where Jeremiah, like Job, also curses the day of his birth and wishes he had never been born (20:14-18). Many of the Psalms are called 'Lament psalms'; the bleakest of which is Psalm 88 which begins in darkness and ends in darkness. Remember that these psalms were part of the worship of the Temple and an important element of Israel's faith. In 2 Corinthians Paul reveals much about the agonies he suffered and in particular his persistent 'thorn in the flesh' (12:7) which he had begged the Lord to take away. The supreme example, however, is our Lord in the Garden of Gethsemane when 'he begun to be deeply distressed and troubled' (Mark 14:33).

This theme is also to be found throughout Christian literature, as witness the following two examples. In *The Dark Night of the Soul* St. John of the Cross expresses it vividly:

> God sometimes attacks the soul in order to renew it and thus to make it God-like, and stripping it of the habitual affections and attachments of the old personality to which it is very closely united, destroys and consumes the spiritual substance, and absorbs it in deep and profound darkness.

A similar emphasis occurs in many of the poems of Gerard Manley Hopkins, especially in his so-called *Dark* or *Terrible* sonnets:

> O the mind, the mind has mountains cliffs that fall, frightful, sheer, no man fathomed. Hold them cheap may they who ne'er hung there ...

The sentence 'Hold them cheap may they who ne'er hung there' is most important. The friends, as we shall see, have 'ne'er hung' where Job is hanging and thus are incapable of empathising with him.

The reference to Hopkins leads to the second general comment on Job 3 which is that it is a poem, indeed it is the beginning of the poetic section of the book which now rolls its majestic way to chapter 41. This means we must respond to it as a poem. It is not enough to take a concordance and look up every reference to darkness and clouds, still less to take a book on meteorology, read the sections on clouds and imagine we have understood this chapter. It must be received as a great poem. Poetry is not a flowery way of saying something which can be said just as effectively in prose. Poetry is a way of expressing the intensest and most powerful emotions in the most concise and compelling way. Thus the distress of Job, and indeed of all who suffer, is encapsulated in this poem of immense and sober power.

In our analysis of this chapter, I want to ask three questions. First: What is the nature of Job's distress? What is actually happening to him? Secondly: What are the reasons for the experience expressed in this poem? Thirdly: Is there a cure for his distress? A cure, that is, suggested by the chapter itself, rather than by jumping to the end of the book.

What is the nature of Job's distress?

The answer is not a straightforward one because many things are happening to him. The first is that his mind and his emotions are utterly dominated by the thought of death. Indeed the theme of death is arguably the dominant one in the book of Job, mentioned as it is in every one of the 42 chapters. Nor is this simply the death of individuals, because, although Job has lost his family, he does not mention them in this chapter. Rather, death is seen as a dark power shadowing the whole of existence. The universe appears to be dominated not by God but by death, which stands as the ultimate question mark over against the goodness of God. The problem is modern as well as ancient and Job powerfully expresses a sense of being gripped and crushed by death.

These feelings of Job are expressed in powerful and colourful images. First of all Job thinks of death as a kind of womb to which he wishes to return. This image has already occurred in 1:21: 'Naked I came from my mother's womb, and naked I shall depart.' The womb and death are the two terminal points and between these are a few years of misery.

Then Job thinks about what might be called the 'geography' of the underworld and his mind is filled with Sheol, the Hebrew name for the world beyond the grave. It is unfortunate that many translations, such as the NIV, do not use the word 'Sheol' but translate it simply as 'grave' or 'death'. Sheol was thought of as a dim, insubstantial, shadowy place where all the activity and all the relationships that mark the world as we know it, ceased.

Job also thinks of death as a place of blackness and shadow: 'May darkness and deep shadow claim it once more' (verse 5). The term 'deep shadow' is the word which is sometimes translated as 'shadow of death' and which is best known from Psalm 23 where the psalmist speaks of 'walking through the valley of the shadow'.

Above all, Job thinks of death as a hostile

presence, an evil spirit dominating his horizon.

But not only are Job's horizon, personality and emotions dominated by death, he is also suffering from what we might call a kind of nihilism: his whole familiar world has simply dissolved around him. There is no longer any meaning and purpose; as the book of Ecclesiastes asserts, everything is vanity, futility, emptiness. The very basis of exist-ence is questioned by Job - what is the point of it all?

Few of us have not been faced with that ques-tion: What is the point of going on? It is sometimes expressed in more colloquial ways: it will all be the same in a hundred years time! We often speak and think what Job, in a much profounder and more poetic way, is expressing in this chapter.

And indeed Job goes further, he wants the whole of creation to be dissolved, the cosmos to dissolve into chaos, the tape to be wound back. If verses 3-10 are read carefully and compared with Genesis 1, Job is wishing that the ancient chaos would return and that it would swallow up the ordered cosmos. God, at the beginning, had said 'Let there be light'; Job says 'May darkness and deep shadow claim it once more.' Genesis 1 is full of vibrant life: the life of animals, fish, birds and of course, the life of humankind itself. Job 3 is full of death. And instead of the Sabbath rest of God satisfied with his work, there is the false rest of Sheol, the dead peace of the graveyard.

Now because of this sense of nihilism, because

of the domination of his thoughts by death, Job has lost his zest for living. Job is not going through a rough patch, something far more profound is happening. Anyone who feels like this knows that being told to get a grip of oneself is simply adding a further cruel pressure. To speak like this is like telling someone with a broken leg to get out of bed and run round the ward. The one thing a person in Job's situation cannot do is to get a grip on himself.

This is illustrated strikingly by a passage which is probably unique: verses 21-22, where Job expresses his passionate desire to break into Sheol the way a grave robber breaks into a tomb. We know from ancient Egypt and elsewhere that there was a profitable trade in grave robbing because of the possessions buried with the dead, but nowhere else does anyone wish to break into Sheol itself. A further illustration of this mood comes from the poetry of the First World War, in the poem *Futility* by Wilfred Owen. In that poem, a young soldier's body lies on the ground in the early Spring sunshine, and the poet muses about his early days, about the sun wakening his every day, even in France, and he ends the poem:

> O what made fatuous sunbeams toil,
> To break earth's sleep at all?

Why did the sun bother setting the whole panorama of life into motion? Thus the nature of Job's distress is that he is dominated by death, nihilism and a lack of zest for living.

What are the reasons for these feelings of despair?

Why has Job apparently lost the robust faith of 1:21 - 'The LORD gave and the LORD has taken away; may the name of the LORD be praised' and the equally robust 2:10 - 'Shall we accept good from God, and not trouble?' Why has he now plunged into the depths of nihilistic despair?

The first reason is this: *the utter silence of his friends*. The last verses of chapter 2, which will be examined later, speak about Job's three friends, Eliphaz, Bildad and Zophar. They come to see him, but very far from comforting him, they treat him as if he were a dead person already. They carry out the rituals of tearing clothes and sprinkling dust which are normally associated with death. They sit and mourn for seven days, and from other parts of the Old Testament we know that this was the common period of ritual morning. Joseph mourned for his father Jacob for seven days; the people of Jabesh Gilead mourned for King Saul, their former saviour, for seven days.

Can you imagine the effect of this on Job? Already crushed and broken, now his friends treat him as if he were already dead, a person without a future, without hope, without anything to look forward to.

Now there is a time for silent sympathy. Sometimes when peoples' hearts are broken, the best thing to do is simply to sit and hold their hands. But there is also a silent bankruptcy when the silence does not arise from sympathising with the person, but from having nothing to say.

This, I suggest, is what is happening here: the friends do nothing, they do not communicate. And this is why the opening verse of Chapter 3 is so important: 'After this, Job opened his mouth.' This is not just an odd way of saying that Job was speaking; it means rather that he was about to say something of significance. The Jerusalem Bible captures the idea very effectively by paraphrasing the phrase, 'Eventually it was Job who broke the silence.' Thus the friends come, and instead of helping they add to the distress.

There is, however, a second element, at a deeper level than the silence of the friends, namely, *the activity of Satan himself*. Some commentators argue that Satan's activity ceases at the end of chapter 2 and that he simply disappears, his task done and he does not feature again. The argument of this whole study, which will be developed in later chapters, is that Satan does not disappear but rather changes guise. Here in chapter 3 he is already at work, filling Job's mind with images of darkness and chaos. We have here the first mention of Leviathan (verse 8), the sea monster and symbol of darkness and evil.

The atmosphere here is rather like that of Shakespeare's *Macbeth* where the witches fill the mind and the dreams of Macbeth with images of death and destruction. Similarly in chapter 7 and elsewhere Job talks about being tormented by dreams and visions. Now what is this all about?

One of the ways the Old Testament, in poetic passages, speaks of creation, is in terms of a battle with the powers of chaos. This theme will be returned to in later chapters but a brief comment is necessary here.

Israel's neighbours in the ancient near east had many myths about a god of order and cosmos destroying a god of chaos usually associated with the raging waters; this is normally related to the creation of the world. Israel's nearest neighbours, the Canaanites, told their sagas of Baal, the champion of the gods, fighting the sea god Yam and the monster Lotan, the Canaanite equivalent of Leviathan. This is not to suggest that the Old Testament revelation is on the same level as the ancient myths, rather that ideas and stories familiar to the people of the time were being used to embody truths.

And there are many places in the Old Testament itself where God's creation of the world is associated with his smiting of hostile powers. One of the most striking of these is Psalm 74:12ff.. In these verses the establishing of the sun and the moon and the making of summer and winter is paralleled by: 'You broke the heads of the monster in the waters.

It was you who crushed the heads of Leviathan.'
Thus God brings cosmos out of chaos.

This dimension of supernatural evil must be
taken seriously. Job is here experiencing what Paul
speaks of in Ephesians 6:12: 'For our struggle is not
against flesh and blood, but against the rulers,
against the authorities, against the powers of this
dark world and against the spiritual forces of evil in
the heavenly realms.' The Satan of chapters 1 and
2 has unleashed spiritual forces against Job and his
whole personality has become a battleground.

But there is another reason, deeper still, why Job
is suffering this distress: *it is the sickening feeling
that God has turned against him.* Verse 20, in most
of the versions, reads 'Why is light given to those
in misery?' Most of the translations and ancient
versions obscure the fact that the Hebrew text says
'Why does he (i.e. God) give light?' Job is placing
the blame fairly and squarely on God.

Then again in verse 23: 'God has hedged in.'
God is no longer seen as protection but as claustro-
phobia. Job has lost his confidence in God and in
God's good purposes for his life. This is also a real
problem for Christians, particularly those who have
been on the journey for some time. Often when
people become Christians, their lives are filled with
joy and peace. The presence of God seems very
close. But then sometimes he appears to withdraw,
and not just withdraw but actually turn against us,
and that is one of the hardest and most poignant

experiences we can ever have. C. S. Lewis, in his
book *A Grief Observed*, which he wrote when his
wife died, expresses just this feeling:

> Meanwhile, where is God? This is one of the
> most disquieting symptoms. When you are
> happy, so happy that you have no sense of
> needing him, so happy you are tempted to
> feel his claims on you are interruption, if then
> you remember yourself and turn to him with
> gratitude and praise, you will be welcomed
> by him with open arms. But go to him when
> need is desperate, when all other help is vain,
> and what do you find? A door slammed in
> your face, and the sound of bolting and dou-
> ble-bolting on the inside. After that silence
> you may as well turn away. The longer you
> wait, the more emphatic the silence becomes.
> There are no lights in the windows; it might
> be an empty house. Was there ever anyone in
> it?

Much of what Job says in the rest of the book is
related to this agony, this feeling that God has
turned against him.

Is there a cure for Job's distress?
If what has already been said about chapter 3 was all
there were to say, it could justifiably be accused of
filling us with bleakness and despair, or at least

reminding us of the bleakness and despair we would prefer to forget. What do we have to place against this? We must avoid the temptation to jump to the end of the book, our concern here is to see if there are any gleams of light in chapter 3 itself. I think two things can be said at this stage.

The first thing is in verse 20: *God gives light*. Now, as we have seen, the fact that God gives light causes Job enormous distress. But this is also to be Job's healing, because what has changed between chapters 2 and 3 is not the fact that God gives light, but the way Job feels about that fact. Job's feelings about God have changed, but the reality of what God is has not changed. Nor has it changed when we ourselves run up against those dreary black times when God appears to have abandoned us, when the powers of darkness are having a field day and when our friends seem at best indifferent and at worst hostile. Then we have to cling to the great unshakeable certainties that God loves, that Christ died, that Christ is risen, that Christ will come again. If these are true, then ultimately it does not matter whether we feel good about them. It is this tension between fact and feeling which lies at the heart of Job's agony.

The second ray of light is *Job's utter honesty*. This is particularly important in two respects. First of all it is important in relation to his thinking and feeling about death. We would do well to remember this too: that we are mortal, that the final truth

about ourselves, about God's care for us and about
our destiny, can never be realised fully in this
world. The final word on an individual can never be
the word that is spoken during one's earthly life.

A missionary returning from long hard work in
central Africa, many years ago in the days of
President Roosevelt, happened to travel across the
Atlantic on the same ship as the President did.
Naturally enough when the ship landed there was
great excitement and an enormous welcoming party
for the President. By contrast there was no-one at
all to welcome the missionary and his wife. That
night in a very modest guest house they would not
have been human if they had not been upset, so as
they prayed they said to God, 'Lord, surely there
might have been at least someone to welcome us
when we arrived home.' And the Lord replied, 'But
you're not home yet.' That makes the point clearly,
the final answer cannot be in this world.

The second feature of Job's honesty is that it
allows God to be honest with him. Not that God is
ever dishonest with us, but sometimes we don't
allow for his honesty. We set up all kinds of
evasions and subterfuges; we try to avoid the truth
and so to avoid him. Job, in contrast to his friends,
realises the supernatural depths of the problem, and
thus God is able to begin the painful process of
healing. At the same time, God is being challenged
by Job about his goodness and providence. We
have to wrestle with this too, as we share Job's

agony and explore the depths with him. And as we explore these depths, if we have the honesty and courage, it will be the doorway for us to meet God in a deeper and fuller way as well.

3

WHEN COUNSELLING DOES NOT HELP
(Job 4-11)

In one of the 'Peanuts' cartoons, Lucy says to Charlie Brown, 'There is one thing you're going to have to learn: you reap what you sow, you get out of life what you put into it, no more and no less.' Now Snoopy the dog who is in the corner of the cartoon doesn't like this much and he mutters, 'I'd kind of like to see a little margin for error.'

Job's friends admit of no margin for error, nor will they allow any deviation from what they see to be the norm.

Having examined the catastrophes which befell Job in the first two chapters, and seen his numbed depression in chapter 3, we realise that if anyone ever needed counselling and support, Job was that man. This is what his friends come to do and yet they merely increase his depression. It is not that counselling in itself is invalid, but that this kind of counselling, where no suspicion or doubt that they might be wrong crosses the minds of the three friends, simply makes Job's situation far worse.

They are like a group of church leaders to whom Oliver Cromwell, having found them to be immov-

ably stubborn, exclaimed in exasperation, 'I be-
seech you by the mercies of Christ, consider that
you may be mistaken.' Job's friends never consider
that they might be mistaken.

The friends stand very comfortably within the
mainstream of the Wisdom tradition with its view
that the life of the righteous leads to prosperity and
happiness. They fail to realise what the Wisdom
literature actually teaches, namely, that when the
book is written, when the final dot is placed on the
page, it will be seen that the life of the just has led
to the perfect day. It does not say anywhere in the
Wisdom books that there will be no tragedies or
disasters en route.

In Psalm 1, for example, which is a concise
summary of what Wisdom is about, the life of the
just is compared to a fruit-bearing tree placed by a
river. There is no suggestion that there will not be
storms or that the tree will not be attacked by
worms; it is simply said that the tree will produce
fruit. What the book of Job does is to fill in the
picture, to explore the implications of the attacks
made on the life of the just.

The three friends are not sharply differentiated
and there is a certain artificiality in trying to write
character studies of them. Nonetheless they do
have certain features which give them some indi-
viduality.

Eliphaz is essentially a philosopher. His characteristic phrases are 'we have examined' and 'I have

observed'. He is the kind of person whom we have all met; the kind of person who knows it all. Whatever you do, whatever you have seen, wherever you have been, he has done it or seen it or been there before you, and if he hasn't, it is because it is not worth going or seeing or doing.

Bildad, on the other hand, is a traditionalist: 'Ask the former generations and find out what their fathers learned' (8:8). He also shows a vindictiveness: 'Your words are a blustering wind.' How is that for making friends and influencing people? Tradition is, of course, important; we cannot simply ignore everything which has ever been said in the past. The trouble with Bildad is that he locates all insight and wisdom in the past and ignores what God is doing now.

Zophar is a dogmatist and a theorist. Even when he speaks about the mystery of God: 'Can you fathom the mysteries of God? Can you probe the limits of the Almighty?' (11:7), he is speaking of the mystery to others, especially to Job, not to himself.

What we are to consider is why the friends fail as counsellors. This is not to be negative, but to explore the positive ways in which counselling can happen and real spiritual help be given. In particular, there are four ways in which the friends fail to counsel adequately and which point beyond themselves to genuine spiritual counselling.

The first thing about the friends is that *they have*

a simplistic and mechanical idea of God. They take ideas about God, about creation, about the world, which are not wrong in themselves, but they apply them in a mechanical and insensitive way. For the situation of Job, as for every other, they have a ready made answer. Eliphaz, for example, says 'You will come to the grave in full vigour, like sheaves gathered in season' (5:26).

This is, of course, what happens at the end of the book. But this does not mean that we can simply jump to the happy ending, scurrying from chapter 2 to chapter 42, as if nothing happened in between. Both Bildad and Zophar argue that since the kind of disasters in chapter 1 do not happen to good people, then Job cannot be good. He must be a secret sinner. Now there are two particular ways in which the friends have a mechanical and simplistic idea of God.

First of all, they have no place in their thinking for a developing relationship with God. This, in effect, is another way of saying that there is no place for a relationship at all, because you cannot have a relationship that does not develop. One of the basic problems of the book of Job is that the friends say all the 'right' things. A reading of chapters 4-27 will demonstrate that the friends speak all the commonplaces of orthodox theology while Job speaks apparently blasphemous words. Yet in 42:7 God says to the friends, 'You have not spoken of me what is right, as my servant Job has.' In other words, God says exactly the opposite of what we expect.

A good example of the exchange between Job and his friends occurs in chapters 15 and 16. Eliphaz, in 15:25,26, says that Job is treating God in the way a warrior treats an enemy: '... he shakes his fist at God and vaunts himself against the Almighty, defiantly charging against him with a thick, strong shield.' In 16:13-14, Job simply turns that on its head: 'Without pity he pierces my kidneys and spills my gall on the ground. Again and again he bursts upon me; he rushes at me like a warrior.'

We have already noticed that this is one of the characteristic ways some of the Old Testament people speak to God. Jacob, for example, in Genesis 32 wrestles with God and refuses to let God go until he has received a blessing. Jeremiah accuses God of seducing him.

The basic problem in our minds, faced with this language of raw hurt and anger, is that we think God is not big enough to handle this kind of thing. We think that God is so delicate, so naive and unsophisticated that he cannot handle this kind of anguish. We also naively think that if we only *feel* that way and do not actually express it in words, God will not know how we are feeling.

Now, of course, once it is put in words, we realise that this is nonsense. Yet there persists in us the feeling that God has to be cocooned and cottonwooled. In fact we treat God as if he were like some fragile maiden aunt who would collapse if we talk about anything outside her limited experience. This comes out in a different way in our hymn-books of all traditions and styles. We major on praise and joy which is right and good in itself. But how many of the lament psalms, for example, do we sing?

Thus the friends don't realise that it is possible to have a developing, at times even an angry, relationship with God. This is true in human relationships. If a relationship goes sour, the way to put it right is not by pretending that nothing has gone wrong. It is usually by hot and angry words that the quarrels of lovers are settled. Pretending that everything is all right simply creates a tense, unreal situation which results in a worse break-up of the relationship.

The other way in which they have a mechanical and simplistic idea of God is that they have no realisation of the dark mystery at the heart of creation itself. Eliphaz urges Job to put his case before God, but Job's basic problem is that he no longer believes God will be just. This is well illustrated in 7:17: 'What is man that you make so much of him, that you give him so much attention?' This is a devastating parody of Psalm 8 where God's care of humanity is seen as a reassuring and strengthening fact. Job does not want care and attention; he wants to be left alone. Thus the friends, because of their simplistic and mechanical view of

God's Providence, do not realise that it is in fact Job's relationship with God which is plunging him into depths of agony and despair.

The second main reason why they fail to be good counsellors is that, like many since, *they imagine they can put God's case better than God*. They appoint themselves as his spokesman, almost as if they don't trust him to put his own case. Much of what they say, taken in isolation, is good, and much of it is echoed by God himself in chapters 38ff., but their basic problem is that they are blind to the majesty of God's creation. They speak about creation and of how important it is to be humble before God, none of which Job disputes, but they miss the point.

Eliphaz in 5:9 says: 'He performs wonders that cannot be fathomed, miracles that cannot be counted.' Job is in no doubt that God can work miracles; it is the good intention of God that he doubts. The idea that God is all-powerful fills him with dread, because in his state of mind he fears this will almost certainly mean further misfortune. Again in chapter 22:12 Eliphaz says: 'Is not God in the heights of heaven? And see how lofty are the highest stars.' His emphasis here is on the all-seeing eye of God and his judgment; once again Job does not doubt this but fears the consequences for himself.

In chapter 11, Zophar speaks about the majesty of creation to say that God can do anything he likes.

The trouble is that this is the very thing Job fears; his problem is that he has lost his faith in the kindness of God. Similarly in chapter 25 Bildad speaks about God's majesty in the heavens, and he ends his tirade with the word 'worm'; man is a worm. Bildad has looked at the sky, he has contemplated the sun, moon and stars and seen nothing more than the reflection of his own sour face. In other words, the majesty of God is simply to keep Job in his place.

Too often, people facing bitter agony and crushing sorrow have simply been beaten into subjection by people who come to the depressed and desolate and tell them rather smugly, 'All things work for good to those who love God.' What is forgotten is that for Paul this hard-won confidence comes at the end of his exposition of the glories of the gospel. This is not said smugly to someone who is suffering agony and trying to hold on to some rags and tatters of their faith; this is said by someone who is himself grappling with the mystery and darkness of creation.

Not only are they impervious to the majesty of God's creation, they are also blind to God's grace. Essentially they hold the view that righteousness leads to prosperity. Today the baneful influence of 'prosperity theology' has deeply infiltrated the church. To put it simply, this kind of theology maintains that if you trust God you will get a good job, a large car and a fine house, you will marry the right person, your children will be wonderful and your material prosperity will prove to the world that God is pleased with you. In other words, God is a bargainer who treats with people on a market basis. Grace goes out of the window and a market economy takes over, where the rich, powerful and successful become the children of the kingdom, and the suffering, the downcast and the oppressed are simply put out. Essentially what the friends are saying to Job is that if he had been genuinely godly his prosperity would have remained.

This imagining that we can make God's case better than God is, of course, the oldest sin in the book. In Genesis 3 that is exactly what Eve did in the Garden of Eden when the serpent tempted her. Eve said that they were allowed neither to eat nor touch the tree. In fact God had said nothing whatever about 'touching' the tree. Eve was making God appear to be strict and tyrannical in order to make it easier to disobey him. She made his *love too narrow by false limits of our own.*' God is misrepresented as someone who bargains instead of someone who pours his grace on us.

The third reason the friends fail as counsellors is because *they do not listen.* The impression given by reading the speeches in the book of Job is that they all come along with prepared speeches which they are going to deliver whatever happens. All with experience of academic or church meetings know how common this is! This is illustrated by the fact that the debate appears to grind to a halt after chapter 25. Zophar does not speak at all; Bildad is uncharacteristically brief, and Eliphaz has fallen silent at the end of chapter 22. Some of the commentaries argue that we have here a dislocation of the speech cycle and they try to rearrange the text among the speakers. I shall comment more fully on this in the discussion of chapter 28, but at the moment it is enough to say that the debate has ground to a halt because no-one has anything else to say. No-one has listened, and consequently they are simply repeating the old tired platitudes.

First of all, *they do not listen to God*. They imagine that they have within themselves all the resources that are required and thus need no new relationship with God. An apparent exception is Eliphaz' dream in 4:12-17 where he speaks of a spirit who spoke to him 'Amid disquieting dreams in the night, when deep sleep falls on men'. This has often been taken as a description of inspiration, but a number of hints suggest that it may in fact have been a brilliant deception by the Evil One. In descriptions of prophetic calls (e.g. Isaiah 6 and Revelation 1) there is indeed fear and trembling; but there is also reassurance and blessing. Moreover, the message, 'Can a mortal be more righteous than God? Can a man be more pure than his Maker' (verse 17), because it is unexceptional, scarcely needs a special revelation from a spirit. There is no hope, no way forward, simply judgment and condemnation.

And that failure is highlighted in another basic failure in counselling. One of the most important lessons to learn in trying to help someone in distress is to take their problem with utmost seriousness. We may privately believe that their perception of their problem is wrong, and we may be right, but in order to help we have to begin with people where they are. The friends come to Job with their minds made up, and thus they are no help to him. Eliphaz rejects anything that does not fit in with his preconceived ideas. Bildad rejects anything that has not been said in the past. Zophar is so fixed in his dogmatism that he has no room for new insights.

Thus not only do they fail to listen to God, *they do not listen to Job in his agony.* At some points in the book Job breaks down. In 13:4 he exclaims: 'You smear me with lies, you are worthless physicians all of you!'; and in 19:21: 'Have pity on me, my friends, have pity, for the hand of God has struck me.' The friends do not perceive the heart of Job's agony, which is not that his prosperity has vanished, but that God appears to have become hostile. As we have seen, this is a common Old Testament problem. Jeremiah, for example, preached for forty years without seeing anyone respond to his preaching. What he said was fulfilled, but it was dreadful and painful and heartbreaking.

We ourselves often fail to listen to the message of suffering. We judge books by whether they make us feel good; we judge worship by whether it makes us happy and we judge people by whether we find them fun and so on. Now that is not to say that it is wrong to read books which make us feel good; nor bad to have worship which is happy, nor unworthy to enjoy the company of amusing people.

What is true is that if all our attention is devoted to these areas we will be like the friends of Job and miss deeper dimensions about God, about suffering and about death. We must listen to God's voice as he speaks through suffering; 'God's megaphone' as C. S. Lewis called it. So often, in the normal business of our lives, the voice of God is almost crushed out; just as sometimes we switch on the radio to a particular channel and we hear faintly and far away the music from another channel. Sometimes that music can become very loud, and sometimes on a personal, community, national or global level, God's megaphone can no longer be ignored and we must listen to what he is saying.

And that brings us to the fourth reason why Job's friends fail as counsellors; *they fail because they do not discern that supernatural forces are at work.* That is not to say that all depression is demonic. Not all agony and suffering comes from the devil, but we must be open to the possibility. This dimension has already been explored in chapter 3 and is further examined in chapter 9. This is precisely the area where many people feel uneasy; they are quite ready to admit in a general sense the existence of

evil powers, but find it difficult to grasp the reality
of their actual involvement in human affairs.

This is the whole point, I believe, of the multitude of references in the book to the powers of death
and chaos which are haunting Job. And this in effect
means that, since the friends cannot attribute suffering and evil to God, they are obliged to argue that
Job has brought it on himself. Jesus warns against
this in John 9 in the incident of the healing of the
blind man. His disciples asked, 'Who sinned, this
man or his parents, that he was born blind?' Jesus
points out that neither is the case. Not that the man
was sinless, but that this blindness was not the result
of a particular evil on his part.

In a sense, of course, what is said about the
attack on Job by demonic powers must be provi-
sional. The Old Testament cannot have a final
answer to this battle with the powers of evil. We
wait for the cross and the resurrection to deal the
death blow to the principalities and powers, and
beyond that to the return of Christ and their final
banishment. But Job has become a grand battleground between the forces of good and evil, and the
whole universe has become a kind of backdrop to
that battle.

The friends fail here as counsellors because
they look only at the superficial; they do not get
alongside Job and they misunderstand the God they
profess to represent. But there is help here for
anyone struggling like Job. God loves, God cares

even if the opposite seems to be true. We need not be afraid to bring our hurt and anger to him. We do not have to pretend we are rejoicing and feeling good or be in anyway dishonest. God understands and cares.

In the final chapter of this book we shall explore further how Christ's victory over Satan gives us a solid foundation for bringing healing into Job-like situations.

4

IF IT IS NOT HE, THEN WHO IS IT?
(Job 9)

At a significant point in *The Lion, the Witch and the Wardrobe*, we read this: 'As Susan heard the strange name, Aslan, she began to tremble, "Oh", said Susan, "is he quite safe?" "Safe?" said Mr. Beaver. "Course he isn't safe. But he's good. He's the king I tell you."'

And that brings us straight to the heart of Job 9. The 'safe' God of chapters 1 and 2 has disappeared; the sunny certainties with which the book begins have vanished and there is a big question which now has to be asked, 'Is he good?' Two observations will help us to focus this.

The first is that in chapter 9 we are facing up to the very heart of what the book is about, which is not just the particular situation of Job and his troubles, but the very nature of God, the mystery of God, the enigma of many of his actions. The chapter is one of tremendous literary beauty and this comes partly from a combination of two types of language. On the one hand, there is hymn-like language: verses 4ff., with their evocation of the majesty of wind, mountain and the starry heavens, that recalls the language of the Psalter. On the other hand, there is the language of the law court. Job is demanding an audience with God; he wants to appear in God's court, to present his case and have himself declared innocent. Verbs such as 'replied' (verse 1); 'dispute' (verse 3); 'answer' (verse 3); 'argue' (verse 14) and 'plead' (verse 15) have distinct legal nuances in Hebrew which are not brought out so clearly in English translations. So the big question is, how can we approach a God like this, and when we have approached him what kind of response will we get?

The second thing to notice is that Job has moved a long way from chapter 3. There Job was sunk in the depths of nihilism and despair; he was in a trap he could not break, a pit he could not climb out of. In the discussion of that chapter it was noted that while the answer did not come there, hints would be discerned of a possible way out: first the conviction that God was behind everything and second the utter honesty with which Job spoke.

But Job here is determined to fight back. He is no longer in a stupefied state where he feels it does not matter and that nothing again will ever matter. He is not going to lie down and take it. He is going to fight back, like Abraham arguing with God to spare the city of Sodom in Genesis 18; like Jacob wrestling with God in Genesis 32.

And Job is asking questions. If we were to be so rash as to select a text which sums up the whole

book of Job, the last part of verse 24 would come as
close to that as any: 'If it is not he, then who is it?'
In this verse Job is actually brushing against the
solution to his problem. If it is not God who is
responsible for all these calamities, then it is possible there may be some sinister force, a power that
can imitate him so cleverly and so subtly as to
appear like God.

Job, then, is wrestling with the question, Is God
good? Linked with that is the question of verse 24:
'If it is not he, then who is it?' We shall examine
how the chapter explores these questions in three
particular spheres. First of all, in the realm of
creation itself, the cosmos in which we live and of
which our earth is part. Second, in the realm of
human society. Third, in relation to his own personal life.

God in creation

Coming first to creation we notice, of course, that
Job is not the first person to speak of creation;
Eliphaz and Bildad have already done so and Zophar
is about to. But the friends, as already noted, had a
totally inadequate idea of God and his creation. In
particular, there are two aspects of Job's attitude to
God and creation which ought to be noted.

There is first of all a sense of wonder and awe.
In the powerful passage verses 3ff., Job creates
images of tremendous power and majesty: imagery
of earthquakes - 'He moves mountains'; images of

darkness - 'He speaks to the sun and it does not shine; he seals off the light of the stars'; images of the great constellations in heaven - 'He is the Maker of the Bear and Orion, the Pleiades and the constellations of the south'.

This sense of wonder is something which is lacking in the speeches of his friends. But it is also significant, and this will be looked at in the discussion of chapter 38, that in places God appears to be echoing Job's words by, for example, mentioning exactly the same constellations as are alluded to here.

Job realises that the solution to his problem does not just lie in himself, there are bigger and profounder issues involved. And this sense of the wonder and vastness of the universe is an integral part of a true relationship with God. Job, although hurt and angry, is using the language of praise, and by using the language of praise he is showing a hunger for God. He still clings to the fact that God is behind everything. The language here, for example, recalls Psalm 46: '... we will not fear, though the earth give way and the mountains fall into the heart of the sea', so what matters ultimately is not changing circumstances, but the greatness and majesty of the Creator.

The second noteworthy feature of Job's response to creation is the sense of order. Indeed behind all response to disaster, whether personal or cosmic, is this desire for order, what the Hebrews

called *shalom*, which means more than peace and
has nuances of harmony and wholeness. This sense
of order is given classic expression in the opening
chapter of Genesis with its description of the days
of creation, the light spreading throughout the
darkness, and the gradual appearance of life in its
multitude of forms. Just as in the cosmos there are
tidal waves, earthquakes and great catastrophes on
an individual and communal scale, so in human life
there are social and personal convulsions.

But in this chapter, the sense of harmony and the
threats to it are referred to in what can be described
as 'mythical' language, which is to become increasingly important in the book. The particular
reference is v. 13: 'God does not restrain his anger;
even the cohorts of Rahab cowered at his feet.' This
is one of the many passages in the Old Testament,
especially in the poetic books, where God's creating activity is expressed in terms of the defeat of the
ancient powers of chaos. These powers are associated with the raging ocean and are sometimes
personified under the names of Leviathan or Rahab.

A number of issues arise here. Why do the
biblical writers use mythical language? What do
we mean by myth? Did the biblical writers actually
believe in these ancient myths? There is a very
helpful discussion of these issues in C. S. Lewis'
essay *Myth Become Fact*; he is not talking specifically about the book of Job, but much of what he

says is relevant to the questions raised here. Lewis
argues that ancient myths are 'good dreams sent by
God to prepare the world for the coming of the
gospel. The gospel is like wakening up out of sleep
to the daylight, but during sleep these myths are
sent as good dreams, and in these myths there are
glimpses of the truth. They are not the full light
which comes in Christ, but they are partial lights'.
He refers to John 1:9: 'The true light that gives light
to every man was coming into the world', and
argues, as some of the Church Fathers argued, that
this means the pre-incarnate Christ enlightened the
whole world in different ways and to different
degrees. Lewis goes on to insist that if we are really
to grasp and be grasped by the gospel we must use
our imagination as well as our minds.

What the Bible writers are doing is using these
images, these pictures from ancient myths, to convey profound truths about the gospel. Myth is an
attempt to embody great ideas in pictorial language. When we use terms such as 'light' and
'darkness', not simply to refer to physical phenom-
ena but to spiritual life and spiritual death, we are
halfway to myth.

In the ancient world there were a number of
legends about light and darkness being embodied in
various figures who battled with each other. In
particular, among Israel's neighbours there were
stories of how the gods of light, order and harmony
defeated the ancient gods of darkness and chaos. It

seems to me that the biblical writers are using this kind of language to suggest, not that the old myths in the form which they appear are true, but that they contain within themselves profound truth: that there is a great struggle at the very heart of creation between light and darkness.

In this sense, *The Lion, the Witch and the Wardrobe* is a modern myth. If we ask, 'Is there a lion called Aslan?'; 'Is there a personality called the White Witch?'; in one sense the answer is 'no'. Yet in another sense the great drama of salvation brings a greater appreciation of the depths and power of the gospel. Lewis is using the old technique of telling a story to convey profound spiritual reality.

So the Old Testament writers use the language of their time, the language people would understand, to convey the reality of the great battle that lies at the very heart of creation, and in which Job has been caught up. This helps us to understand the references to Rahab and Leviathan. Job realises that his tragedies are supernatural in origin. He is aware of these powers. What he is not yet aware of is that God is able to use these powers in his total creation. This, incidentally, receives fascinating confirmation from modern physics which speaks of 'Chaos theory' and argues that in the whole of the creative process, chaos can form an integral part and be bound up in the act of creation. In other words, such is the creating power of God that even chaos can be brought into the overall picture.

On a spiritual level the Old Testament is saying that the ancient power of chaos, the Satan himself of Job 1 and 2, is ultimately as Luther called him, 'God's devil', and ultimately his evil purposes will be woven into God's good creative purposes in such a way that even Satan in the last analysis will have to do God's will. Paul says this explicitly in Romans 8:28 'All things (presumably including such things as persecution, peril, sword, principalities and powers) work together for good to those who love God' (AV). Paul does not say that everything is in itself good. What he says is that in God's loving purposes all these things ultimately result in goodness, and it is a dim awareness of this that Job is showing in his sense of the order of creation. So then, Job has this sense of wonder, this sense of order, and he dimly glimpses that behind the awful things happening to him lurk the powers of evil, but behind them stands the God of chapters 1 and 2.

God and society

With that in mind, we look now at the second area, which is Job's concern for society. This comes out particularly in verse 22: 'It is all the same; that is why I say, "He destroys both the blameless and the wicked".' This is developed in the following two verses in more specific ways. This shows that even in his agony he is not self-centred. He is in the depths of despair, sitting on this ash-heap, his health ruined, his family gone, his prospects blighted; and even in these circumstances he still has what we would call a social conscience. He still cares deeply about others and the state of society.

It is worth noting first of all his sense of justice. Just as *shalom* is vital for the cosmos, so it is vital in human societies. The order of the cosmos is to be reflected in the order of human society. That is classic 'Wisdom' teaching as it is presented especially in the book of Proverbs. If Satan is causing chaos in creation, then that chaos will be reflected in society as well. The whole of the cosmos, including the human part, will be affected, and the natural tendency will be to place this at God's door. This is illustrated by a most poignant story.

A man was going to see his little daughter who was dying of cancer in hospital. He was taking her a cake because it was her birthday, and on the way he stopped to go into a church and pray. He prayed very hard before the altar that God would spare his little daughter's life. When he got to the hospital he found that his child had died a few minutes earlier. If he had not stopped to pray he would have been with her when she died. He did not say, 'The Lord gave and the Lord has taken away, blessed be the name of the Lord'. He rushed back to the church and flung the cake at the crucifix on the altar. Who can blame him? This is an outpouring of scalding agony. And this is how Job is feeling here and why he is demanding that God should explain himself. And, of course, the whole point of the book is that

God is big enough to take this. Job's friends, however, are not big enough to take it. Their God is not big enough to take it either and they think that they have to protect him against that kind of anger. The capacity to be outraged is one of the signs of a sense of justice and fairness.

The second aspect of Job's concern for society is his own example. This comes out particularly clearly in chapter 29 which gives a moving and vivid picture of Job's life as it would have been in chapter 1, before all these calamities happened. He not only gives a clear picture of the respect and affection in which he was held, but demonstrates above all his concern for the poor and disadvantaged, the widows and fatherless. In the Old Testament righteousness always has a social dimension and covenant is always seen in terms of community. This is clearly seen, for example, in Amos and in the opening chapters of Isaiah. Being righteous always includes caring for the ills of society.

Job exemplifies this, and the interesting thing is that God himself never disputes this at any point, and thus we have no reason to believe that Job was telling anything other than the truth. He builds up a picture of personal integrity and social justice which is very much the kind of thing commended to us in the letter of James; and, of course, James actually mentions the endurance of Job as one of his examples of righteousness. Yet in chapter 30 we have a complete contrast: the world that he now lives in is a world of desolation, brokenness and chaos; his grief is profound and his indignation burns.

God and Job

This brings us to the third area of chapter 9, which is Job himself. In this chapter, particularly in the last verses, Job has an uneasy combination of, on the one hand, a longing to meet God and, on the other, extreme terror at the prospect, just as Susan in Narnia was both afraid of encountering Aslan and yet desperate to meet him.

It is important to notice Job's sense of innocence. This is perfectly genuine and we must remember that nowhere does God accuse Job of secret sin. Job's fear is not that he is guilty, but that even his goodness will not help him in any kind of way that matters before God. Even human goodness will not grant him a satisfactory hearing.

There is also a sense of transience. This is brilliantly encapsulated in three similes of increasing speed: a swift runner (verse 25); a papyrus boat skimming across the water (verse 26); and an eagle swooping on its prey (verse 26). A similar scene is evoked in a famous passage in Bede's *Ecclesiastical History* where a missionary speaks at the court of King Edwin of Northumberland and compares the life of humans to a sparrow that flies into the lighted hall for a moment, lingers in the warmth and then flies out into the darkness beyond. This is basic to the human condition; the sense of the inexorable and swift passage of time.

Finally there is Job's longing for an arbiter, which we shall explore further in the next chapter: 'If only there were someone to arbitrate between us, to lay his hand upon us both' (verse 33). This is a leap of faith, which occurs again in chapters 16 and 19. Here the identity of this arbitrator is not specified, yet the faint hope has been kindled in Job's heart that there might be someone in the heavenly court who will stand up and speak for him.

I think that in this dim, shadowy figure we have one of the Old Testament intimations of the Advocate in heaven, the Advocate who is both one with God and one of us, the Advocate who is going to put his hand on both. This is why it is so important to have a correct understanding of who Jesus actually is. He is not the ideal specimen of humanity standing at the head of the rest of us, to whose coat tails we hang, as it were, while he stretches out his hand to touch God. Jesus is the hand of God stretching out across the gulf to raise us to His presence. And this individual on his ash-heap, in bitter anger and in desperate agony, glimpses the heart of the gospel, an Advocate who can lay his hand on both him and God.

5

TO WHOM CAN WE TURN?
(Job 19)

A friend was on a walking holiday on the island of Skye with a friend of his who is an atheist, and my friend, who is a Christian, said, 'When you are a Christian, everything is different, you just step out in faith and God looks after you.' Well, he stepped out in faith and landed up to his middle in a peat bog!

Job, by this stage in the book, is up to his neck, not in a peat bog, but in a pit of depression and he is sorely in need of a helping hand. He is desperately needing what is called here in chapter 19, a 'redeemer' - the Hebrew word is *go'el* which is difficult to translate and contains ideas of 'saviour', 'advocate' and much else.

This passage has, of course, been immortalised by Handel's music. At root is the question which Job has been asking with increasing intensity: 'How can we have a relationship with God who causes the innocent and the good to suffer?' Now this is not a question to which there is a slick and easy answer, some convenient phrase which will make everything all right. These problems have to be wrestled with intellectually, emotionally and spiritually.

Job, in his battling with these questions, has moved on and he is no longer exactly where he was in chapter 9. There is an increasing desperation in what he says and an increasing vindictiveness in what the friends say. In the earlier speeches, the friends tended to talk in generalisations, rather vague statements about the good and the bad, but now they have become much more specific and extremely hurtful and vindictive. For example, in chapter 18, Bildad presents a grisly and gruesome picture of the fate of the wicked by whom he clearly means Job. Since, according to Bildad, the good do not suffer and the wicked do, Job must belong to the wicked. Job, therefore, feels that he needs to be vindicated; the longing for an advocate is becoming more desperate than ever. Indeed, he wants to have a permanent record of his thoughts and feelings: 'Oh, that my words were recorded, that they were written on a scroll, that they were inscribed with an iron tool on lead, or engraved in rock for ever!' (19:23,24).

Three questions need to be addressed: Why particularly at this point does Job need a mediator? Who is that mediator? What will be the result of the mediator's activities?

Why at this point does Job need a mediator?
In one sense, the answer is obvious: he needs a mediator because he is harassed and persecuted

beyond endurance. But there are two factors which make the need especially great.

The first is that *Job is increasingly conscious that God is attacking him*. In 16:9ff., he speaks of this in extremely vivid and startling language: 'God assails me and tears me in his anger and gnashes his teeth at me'; and again, 'All was well with me, but he shattered me; he seized me by the neck and crushed me'. And yet, as we shall see, this very sense of being attacked by God is the reverse side of Job's desperate need for God. It is all so hurtful because he needs God badly and loves him deeply.

More especially, the recent chapters have been dominated by death, culminating in 18:14 with Bildad's picture of the 'king of terrors'. And it is this area, of course, which raises the problem most acutely: what if Job dies unvindicated? What if he goes to his grave with his name denigrated, with all he has gone through and with nothing to show that God cares?

Job, in this chapter, describes God's attacks on him in a series of vivid pictures (verses 7-12). He is an individual alone and attacked; somebody mugged in a city and calling for help while people pass by unheeding. Then he thinks of a traveller on a blocked road as night falls. There are also pictures of buildings destroyed and trees uprooted. Most devastating of all is the image of Job in his pathetic little tent, being besieged by God's enormous armies. God is attacking him and he needs to be defended.

The second element is his sense of alienation from others which he sees as God's fault: 'He has alienated my brothers from me; my acquaintances are completely estranged from me. My kinsmen have gone away; my friends have forgotten me.' God is not only attacking Job directly, but has turned everyone against him. This is often a painful fact of our experience: we feel that everyone has abandoned us, that nobody cares and that God himself has become hostile.

There is a good illustration of this in Mark 5. Jairus, a synagogue ruler, goes to Jesus in great distress and says, 'My little girl is critically ill, will you come and help her.' Instead of helping immediately, Jesus stops to heal someone else whose need is apparently less great, and during that delay Jairus' world crashes about his ears: 'Jairus don't bother the Teacher any more, she's dead.' At this point Jairus must have felt that even Jesus didn't care. It is to this desperate man that Jesus responds with words which are simple but strangely powerful, 'Don't be afraid, trust me'. That is what Jairus must hang on to in that dark moment.

Job too is desperately searching for someone he can trust. He needs a mediator because of the apparent hostility of God and because people have turned against him.

Who is the mediator?

We must remind ourselves of the basic situation of
the book of Job. Job is not suffering because of a
series of accidents. These events have had their
origin in the heavenly court and have been orchestrated by God himself. We noticed that Job had in
fact glimpsed this: 'If it is not he (God), then who
is it?' (9:24). In that same chapter he has spoken of
an 'umpire' (verses 32-35) '... someone to arbitrate
between us, to lay his hand upon us both ...'(verse
33).

At that point, this figure is shadowy and ill-
defined. But once this hope has been expressed it
cannot simply be left at that. Once Job has expressed the hope, distant, even crazy as it might
seem, it has to be built on, it has to be taken up. In
a real sense that is true of the whole Old Testament.
The faint hope is growing clearer all the time, and
an increasing longing is expressed for someone in
whom all God's purpose will be embodied: 'God's
presence and his very self'. The hope grows clearer
and becomes more defined in 16:19 where Job says:
'Even now my witness is in heaven; my advocate is
on high.' In a leap of faith, Job almost has a vision
of the heavenly court, and he catches a glimpse of
someone who can put his case for him.

Job here, I think, is glimpsing the greatest paradox of the Christian faith, whereby it almost appears to us as if there are two Gods - a God of
judgment and a God of love. That is often what our

experience seems to demonstrate. Sometimes God shows such love toward us that we wonder why we ever doubt him; at other times he seems to turn on us with such flinty hostility that we wonder why we ever trust him. In these latter situations God's enemy is masquerading as God and making it appear that God is the Attacker. Job is terrified by this God who is hurting him so badly, but even in his hurt he remembers the good and kindly God of chapters 1 and 2 and strives to understand the paradox.

Who then is this *go'el*? In the Old Testament the word is used of God as champion of the oppressed and as kin to Israel. Sometimes the word has been rendered as 'kinsman-redeemer'. God, in other words, is more than Israel's redeemer, he stands in a specific relationship to them. In Numbers 35 we read of the '*go'el* of blood', sometimes called the 'avenger of blood', whose duty was to seek out and kill someone who had murdered a member of his family.

Indeed, in ancient Judaism, many of the matters which are now dealt with by the courts were handled within the family. Everything to do with marriage, for example, was a matter for the head of the family. The best example of this in the Old Testament is the book of Ruth, where Boaz not only helps Ruth, the girl from Moab, but actually marries her. The *go'el* was far more than an advocate in the legal sense, he was someone who stood in an

organic relationship to those he helped. The verbal
form of *go'el*, often translated 'vindicate', is used
often of God rescuing his people from Egypt and
from other oppressors. In many ways it is close to
the word *paracleitos* in the New Testament, which
refers to the Holy Spirit and emphasises relationship as well as representation.

Is this *go'el*, then, God himself? Many commentators argue that it cannot possibly be God
because God is the judge. How can the judge also
be the defence counsel? Normally, of course, that
would be impossible, but that is to misunderstand
the thrust of the book. If it is God who is being
accused of doing the attacking, and if a *go'el* is
someone who represents the weak and the helpless
against the strong, then who but God can negotiate
with God?

What will be the result of the mediator's activities?
Granted that Job needs a *go'el* because of God's
perceived hostility, and granted that the *go'el* in the
last analysis can be no other than God himself, what
will happen? Two matters are worth noting.

First of all, this *go'el* will stand on the earth,
stand on the dust (verse 25). These lines are obscure
in Hebrew and the subject of intense debate. Is this
a glimpse of life beyond death? The letter to the
Hebrews speaks of this in relation to Abraham and
others who were looking for a city whose building
and architect is God (11:10). The writer goes on to

say that they were looking for a better country, a heavenly one (11:16). Is Job here catching a glimpse of the promised land?

To talk of heaven is to risk being labelled 'other-worldly' and be the butt of snide remarks: 'too heavenly-minded to be of any earthly use' - not that I have ever met anyone in my life like that. But the point is that heaven is not an optional extra, heaven is the unveiled presence of God. And it seems what has happened here is that for a moment the world beyond has broken into Job's world. Surrounded as he is by negative images, the life of the world to come has for a moment shone into his darkness. Charles Wesley speaks of this in one of his greatest hymns: 'I woke, the dungeon flamed with light.'

Job's dungeon does not exactly flame with light, but a ray of light has penetrated, a key has clanked in the door; there is hope, there is dawn beyond the night. God, he says, will stand on the 'dust'. The Hebrew word *'apar* used here means 'dust' rather than 'the earth' and, in the poetic books of the Old Testament including Job itself, is often used in the sense of 'grave'. Is this a picture of the *go'el* trampling underfoot the power of death? Obviously that is an idea which cannot come into prominence in the Old Testament. It awaits the Resurrection and the Empty Tomb. Yet it is one of the Old Testament glimpses of the final victory over death and the power of the grave. In this moment of agony, Job glimpses someone, beyond this world and this life, who will stand on the dust and trample underfoot all the negative and hostile forces which are ranged against him.

The second prominent note in this passage is the emphasis on 'seeing' God. Job says: 'in my flesh I will see God; I myself will see him with my own eyes - I, and not another' (verses 26-27).

Many commentators argue that this means his vindication will come while he is still alive. This is, of course, true in itself. In 42:5 Job says 'My ears had heard of you but now my eyes have seen you'. The phrase 'in my flesh' - i.e. while I am still in my body - could equally be translated 'from my flesh' or 'out of my flesh' - i.e. when I have gone from my body, when I have left this world. In a real sense this does not matter; the important thing is not when and where he sees God, but that he will see God. And that is what Christian living is about. In the book of Revelation, where in image after image heaven has been summoned up, a phrase in the final chapter crystallises it all: 'His servants will serve him. They will see his face' (22:3,4).

This is wonderfully expressed in a passage towards the end of *The Screwtape Letters* where Screwtape writes to Wormwood in baffled rage at how at the moment of death their 'patient' had entered life everlasting:

One moment it seemed to be all our world, the scream of bombs, the fall of houses, the

stink and taste of high explosive on the lips
and in the lungs; the feet burning with wea-
riness, the heart cold with horrors, the legs
aching, the brain reeling. Next moment all
this was gone: gone like a bad dream. Defeated, outmanoeuvred fool, did you mark
how naturally the earth-born vermin entered
the new life?

Then this:

He saw him. This animal, this thing begotten
in a bed, could look on him. What is blinding,
suffocating fire to you is now cool light to
him, is clarity itself and wears the form of a
man.

'He saw him'; that is the ultimate answer to Job's
and to all our tragedies.

6

WHERE CAN WISDOM BE FOUND?
(Job 28)

There can be no doubt that Job has travelled a long way since the agonies of chapter 3, and that the *go'el* passage in chapter 19 has marked a significant breakthrough, an enormous leap of faith in the darkness. Much more ground has still to be travelled, though, and there is to be no immediate easing of Job's situation. Indeed, the immediate response to Job's speech is a particularly vindictive tirade by Zophar which includes a grisly description of how the wicked will meet their fate. This is followed by a more measured, but no less condemnatory speech by Eliphaz in chapter 22, which is a legal indictment of Job as a wicked man and a summons to him to repent.

To these Job replies in chapters 23 and 24 with an impassioned appeal for a hearing in the heavenly court and, in chapter 24, an eloquent appeal for justice for the poor and needy. Many have argued that the second part of this chapter (24:18-25) cannot be by Job because it appears to be diametrically opposed to his claim in chapter 21 that the innocent suffer and the guilty prosper. Chapter 24 claims, as the Friends do, that punishment for the wicked is inevitable and inexorable. But Job has never disputed that God will judge the wicked, what he has maintained is that he is not one of them. This is the thrust of verse 25: 'If this is not so, who can prove me false and reduce my words to nothing?' Thus there is no need to attribute this part of the speech to Zophar or Bildad.

That illustrates a wider problem of this whole section of the book which contains the majestic poem to wisdom in chapter 28, our main subject in this chapter. What is the relation of this poem to the surrounding chapters, especially 24-31? What is its purpose in the developing argument of the book, especially in relation to God's speeches in 38-41? We shall first of all explore the context, then look at the arguments of the chapter itself, and finally reflect on the issues raised by this presentation of wisdom.

We have plainly reached a stage in the book of Job where the debate is running into trouble and the reader is wondering if the gigantic problems raised are going to be solved. Chapter 28 appears out of place with its calm and measured tone, compared with the frenetic speeches surrounding it. The text as it stands appears to regard the chapter as part of a speech by Job, and yet 26-31 seems inordinately long for such a speech, and the lack of speeches of reply by the Friends, except for the uncharacteristically brief speech of Bildad in chapter 25, have led many commentators to reassign and rearrange the chapters. My argument is that chapters 26-31 have an essentially choric function and bring together much of the theology and imagery of the earlier chapters, thus providing a secure basis for the divine speeches where all these matters are definitively addressed.

It may be also that the characters have run out of things to say. Zophar sputters out in angry silence in chapter 20, and Job turns his words against him in 27:13-23. Similarly, Eliphaz, in chapter 22, gives a legalistic indictment (much of which Job answers in chapters 29-31) and what he says sounds like the final summing-up of a prosecuting counsel. Bildad peters out in sour and patronising commonplaces. The poet is plainly suggesting that a new and outside initiative is needed; none of them have the answer.

What he does is provide us with an overview of the imagery and themes of the book which both summarises the journey already travelled and points forward to the next stage. Chapter 26 encapsulates the wonders and mysteries of creation and cosmic evil. Indeed, this can be seen as another of Job's leaps of faith, because the structure of what he says anticipates the thrust of God's own speeches in chapters 38-41. 26:1-4 are a challenge, which God answers in chapter 38 when he begins to speak; verses 5-10 correspond to chapters 38-39 with their evocation of the mysteries of the universe; and verses 11-14 refer to the mystery of supernatural evil which is the thrust of chapters 40-41. Thus Job is showing that openness to God which is at the heart of any true relationship with him.

Chapter 27 turns to legal imagery and the court scene with the adversary, a vivid reminder of chapters 1-2. We have moved from God's power to his justice, and Job's reference to the 'works' of God (26:14) have reminded him forcibly of the mystery of Divine Providence and his inability to explain these ways. Job uses the words of the Friends against them and speaks of calamities in human rather than cosmic terms. Thus the emphasis is on starving children, destitute widows and loss of home and possessions.

Leaving chapter 28 aside for a moment, we glance at 29-31 which is Job's final summing-up of the case for his innocence. Chapter 29 paints a vivid picture of a peaceful and harmonious society which reflects the ordered government of the universe unfolded in chapter 28. Chapter 30 shows, by contrast, images of deprivation and terror and thus draws on the dark side of the mystery of God's ways in creation. Moreover, like chapter 3, it contains images of 'uncreation', e.g. light turning to darkness (verse 26). Chapter 31 represents the culmination of the legal language in the speech cycles with Job's protestations of innocence and purity. The emphasis is on inner attitudes rather than outward actions. Job, in the closing verses, argues that he is in tune with nature and thus his case deserves an answer.

It is in this context that I examine chapter 28 and its exploration of the theme of Wisdom. The chapter can conveniently be divided into three parts: verses 1-11 the search for wisdom illustrated by mining; verses 12-22 the inaccessibility of wisdom; verses 23-28 wisdom and creation. Since the chapter is a kind of pause for breath and reflection, we shall not be surprised to find many echoes of the journey thus far, as well as anticipations of what is to come.

The search for wisdom (verses 1-11) draws on the dangers and challenges of mining to illustrate the formidable difficulties in the search for wisdom. The vivid and tangible nature of the description reminds us that the sorrows of Job had not merely been in his mind, but had been very real and palpable. Job is in the blackest darkness and is assailed by a crushing sense of isolation.

A second feature of this section is the theme of probing and searching: wisdom will not yield her secrets easily. This is underlined by the commodities mentioned in verses 5-6: bread with all the process of sowing, reaping and the sustaining of life; and precious stones with suggestions of costly effort. Thus there is the strong implication that the effort to find wisdom will be equally costly.

Mere human wisdom and achievement are not condemned, any more than Job's wealth and happiness were in the Prologue. Verse 1, about the refining of gold, plainly echoes 23:10: 'When he has tested me, I shall come forth as gold.' That chapter, as well, contains the idea of diligent and passionate searching for God. Thus the picture of mining reflects Job's search for the Divine wisdom which lies behind creation.

The question implied in comparing the search for wisdom to mining is now addressed in the second section (verses 12-22) on the inaccessibility of wisdom. The key words 'wisdom' and 'understanding' are to be taken up by God in chapters 38 and 39 and put into their proper perspective. This chapter is an anticipation of that and a powerful reminder that all human searching and exploring is futile without God's gracious revelation. In verses 13-14 it is stated that wisdom cannot be found by ransacking the material or human universe. We may find glimpses of it, but wisdom itself still eludes us. We are being prepared for the awesomeness of God's own speeches and the proper humility of realising our own smallness in the scheme of things.

Wisdom, like love in the Song of Songs 8:7, cannot be bought. The richest treasures of the exotic east are weighed in the balance against wisdom and found wanting. We are being forced gradually into a recognition of the severe limitations of human power and understanding. Even in the realms beyond human understanding - the

pathless heavens and the realms of destruction and
death - no real trace of wisdom can be found.

In the final section (verses 23-28) it is interesting to note that Wisdom is scarcely mentioned;
rather it is God's power in creation which is celebrated. This emphasis on creation is seen in verse
23: 'God understands the way to it and he alone
knows where it dwells.' God knows because he is
the Creator and he 'sees' because it is from his own
mind and heart that he creates. True seeing by
mortals is thus a gift from God and requires his
revelation of himself. This is exactly what God is
shortly to do for Job when he takes him on a tour of
the wonders of the universe.

The details of creation in verses 25-26 are full of
interest. The poet selects those details - wind, rain,
lightning and thunder - which are generally seen as
the most elusive and unpredictable, and shows how
they are governed by fixed patterns: 'When he
made a decree for the rain and a path for the
thunderstorm'. Moreover these are the very forces
in nature which are ambiguous and are both life-
giving and destructive, which exactly demonstrates
the riddle about the ways of God which is at the
heart of the book.

This section is summed up in verses 27 and 28.
Verse 27 is a general statement about creation and
the wisdom which is at its heart. The full implications of this verse are still to be explored in chapters
38 and 39. Once again the importance of 'seeing'

is underlined, reminding us of Job's leap of faith in
19:26-27:

> ... in my flesh I will see God;
> I myself will see him
> with my own eyes ...

and pointing forward to 42:5:

> My ears had heard of you,
> but now my eyes have seen you.

In Genesis 1, God looks on his creation and
pronounces it 'good', and in Job, God's seeing
includes 'confirming' and 'testing', words which
have implications of probing and exploring; God is
telling Job that there are depths and mysteries in the
universe of which he knows nothing.

Verse 28 stands somewhat apart from the poem
with its introductory phrase 'and he said to human
beings'. This is a reminder that the message of this
book is wider than the specific situation of Job
himself. Wisdom is not theoretical and the most
rigorous search will not find it, yet there is a way to
experience it. That way is 'the fear of the LORD'
exemplified by Job in chapter 1. The use of 'LORD'
is probably deliberate, recalling the Prologue and
anticipating God's own speeches.

We are now in a position to reflect on the issues
raised by this chapter at this point in the book. The

journey we have travelled has mirrored much of
human experience as it wrestles with the mysteries
of living and dying. Chapters 1 and 2 give us the
story on its different levels: the rapid unfolding of
the catastrophes which reduce Job's world to dust
and ashes, and the orchestration of these events in
the heavenly court. This emphasised the need for
vision to penetrate behind the outward events. This
was followed by the numb despair of chapter 3 and
the inadequacy of the Friends as counsellors. Then
the dialogue unfolds with its blend of angry protest,
misunderstandings, claim and counterclaim. This
is a necessary journey to travel: the dark night must
be lived through, the hard questions asked, the great
issues grappled with.

Chapter 28 is thus a vital pause and, with its calm
and measured tone, it invites reflection. The themes
and images of the chapter are brilliantly used to
further the flow of the book. The description of
mining not only suggests suffering and solitude,
which mirrors Job's plight, but also evokes the
mysteries of the underworld. Moreover, there is a
profound admiration of human ingenuity which is
in stark contrast to Bildad's sour dismissal of humans as 'maggots' (25:6); yet it also shows human
limitations: with all our powers we are unable to
find wisdom.

The 'debate', however, has ground to a halt with
the Friends becoming ever more condemnatory,
and while Job has shown astonishing insight at

some points (e.g. chapters 9 and 19), chapter 27 has shown that his insight has proved ineffective as a bulwark against depression. Thus, here in chapter 28, a statement of the fundamental wisdom and order underlying the universe is necessary and allows a breathing space for passions to subside. Job's long speech (chapters 29-31) is a final summing-up for the defence, in which he gives his reasons for claiming that he has in fact walked in 'the fear of the LORD'.

Three comments conclude our consideration of chapter 28. The first is that the chapter is a theological consideration of the place of wisdom in creation, and one which ranges from the depths of the earth to the furthest reaches of sea and sky. Theology is necessary: we must think large thoughts about God, creation and humanity. Yet theology on its own is not enough (we shall explore this further in our consideration of the Elihu speeches), and only hearing God and seeing him will address the huge issues raised in the book. Theology, properly used, is a step along that way.

Secondly, this chapter has a realistic view of human potential and limitations. The view of humanity which emerges is firmly in line with the general thrust of Old Testament teaching. In Genesis 1:26-27 where the creation of humans occurs, the word *ba'ra* (to create), only ever used in the Bible of God, is used three times, having been sparingly employed in the previous verses. Yet

humans are not the whole of creation, they are
given only part of the sixth Day! Similarly, in
Psalm 8 humans are 'a little lower than the angels'
yet insignificant under the awesome beauty of the
starry heavens. Here in Job 28 the considerable
achievements of humans are celebrated: the penetrating into the remote recesses of the earth; the
wrestling of its treasures from the soil; the geo-
graphical and cosmological discoveries.   Yet
wisdom and the control of the elements are far
beyond man, and the mysteries at the heart of
creation are outside his knowledge.

Finally, 'the fear of the LORD' can never simply
be a matter of theory, as if grasping it by the mind
meant that we now *know* what wisdom is. The
parallel phrase 'to shun evil' shows that the whole
way of life is involved. Proverbs 3:7 states 'Do not
be wise in your own eyes; fear the LORD and shun
evil'. This has been true of Job as outlined by the
narrator in chapter 1, and is to be developed by Job
in his defence in chapters 29-31. So we are still
waiting for an answer: why has this wise man been
treated thus?

7

TRYING TO TIE HIM DOWN
(Job 32-37)

Many years ago I heard an evangelistic sermon
preached from Job 36:18. In the Authorised Ver-
sion this reads: 'Because there is wrath, beware lest
he take thee away with his stroke: then a great
ransom cannot deliver thee.' Incidentally, most of
the modern versions translate it differently. The
sermon was good in itself (the fact it is still remem-
bered after a lapse of years proves that!) and its
point that God in Christ had 'paid the price for sin'
to prevent us being banished from his presence is,
of course, glorious truth.

However, that sermon could just as well, indeed
more appropriately, have been preached from the
letter to the Romans, and I mention it here to show
the dangers of taking verses out of context. The
sermon gave to Elihu's words an authority they do
not have in their context, because his words, like
those of all the other speakers, have to be judged by
God's own words in chapters 38-41, and by the
final part of the story in chapter 42. Seen in this
light, Elihu's contribution is found wanting. To be
truly biblical in our thinking we must take books as

a whole and listen to their distinctive message and not simply fillet them for texts which illustrate the distinctive message of other biblical books.

It is true that Elihu says many good things and we shall look at these, but the flaw behind all that he says is that it is theoretical and lacks pastoral warmth. I have already mentioned C S Lewis' powerful book *A Grief Observed*, written when his wife died. Many years before this, Lewis wrote one of his fine apologetic works *The Problem of Pain* which wrestles bravely and honestly with the mystery of suffering in a world created and sustained by a loving God. Lewis makes many valid and penetrating points, but whereas his later book springs from intense personal grief, this earlier one has the atmosphere of the study and debating chamber. That is right and valuable in its place but is no cure for the black depression and broken heart of someone like Job. Elihu's contribution is long on theology and short on pastoral concern.

So it is that Elihu tries to tie God down and give to Job a theology of creation and suffering which fails to address the real issues. Elihu speaks at great length and there is a fair amount of repetition in what he says. Many commentators, indeed, have dismissed these chapters (32-37) as a later interpolation which is seen, in literary terms, as inferior to the rest of the book and lacking in real power. It is further pointed out that he is introduced abruptly and is not heard of again. Most strikingly of all, God simply ignores his contribution. That view, I think, misunderstands the significance of the Elihu passage. The poetry of the speech is indeed inferior to the magnificence of 38-41, but surely we would expect the best poetry to be reserved for God! Moreover, the fact that God ignores him is rather a comment on the fact that he is to be taken simply as another character in the drama, and not on his own terms as adjudicator and arbiter. So what we shall do is first, look at Elihu himself; then, make some comments on the substance of what he says; and finally, reflect on the significance of these chapters in the book of Job as a whole.

Elihu

Elihu is introduced by a prose prologue (32:1-5) which is a characteristic device of the book. Thus we are coming to a new stage in the action. As we noticed in our discussion of the Wisdom poem (chapter 28) the contribution of the Friends has run into the sand. Chapter 31:40 has stated 'The words of Job are ended.' The Friends have failed to provide an answer and Job's conviction of his own righteousness has not been shaken. It is at this point that Elihu assumes the mantle of arbiter and proceeds to give his exposition of what he sees as the reality of the situation. He has clearly listened to the previous dialogue and, as we shall see, there are many references and allusions to what the other characters have said.

It is worth noticing the way in which the author skilfully suggests how we are to regard Elihu's contribution by deftly pointing out features of his personality.

First of all, he is presented as an angry young man. Four times we are told that Elihu is angry, not perhaps the most promising way to begin what purports to be an authoritative disclosure of the ways of God. He is also shown as egocentric (32:10: 'Therefore I say: listen to me'; 32:17: 'I too will have my say').

And what is more, this cleverly underlines the difference between Elihu's self-image and the way he actually appears. There is a patronising tone about all he says and he uses the technique of superficial respect to be scathingly dismissive of others. He uses the language of modesty to disguise arrogance. Many of the things Elihu says may well be right, but he himself is no good example of his words.

The argument of Elihu

With this in mind, then, let us look at the substance of what he says. In chapters 32 and 33 he uses the legal language we have become so familiar with throughout the book of Job. At first sight he seems to have a wider vision than the Friends whom he castigates for their failure to answer Job: 'But not one of you has proved Job wrong; none of you has answered his arguments' (32:12). But his fire is equally directed against Job. He criticises the Friends for leaving it to God to refute Job (32:14), but that is exactly what is to happen, although in a way that Elihu could not even begin to imagine. This is followed by windy rhetoric in verses 15-22, which for all its high flown vocabulary amounts to the claim that Elihu is bursting to say something.

What he does say summons Job to a formal hearing in court: 'Answer me then, if you can; prepare yourself and confront me' (33:5). In verses 8-11 Elihu draws from various speeches of Job (e.g. 9:20, 21; 27:5,6 and 31:6). Then he specifically turns to Job's often repeated complaint that God will not give him a hearing. After the elaborate build up we are hardly set alight by his statement (verse 12) that 'God is greater than man', undoubtedly true, but scarcely an original contribution! He then speaks of various ways in which God does speak to humans: by dreams (verses 15-18), by sickness (verses 23-28) and by healing (verses 23-28).

None of this can be disputed, but the very point of the book is that Job does not know what God is saying to him through his sickness and other calamities. As for dreams, these have been an added burden: 'You frighten me with dreams and terrify me with visions' (7:14). One of the important things the writer is doing in the Elihu speech is reminding us of many of the things that Job has said just before God answers them.

Chapter 34 is set in the world of courts and litigation. Elihu sets out a defence of God's government of the universe. Here he is responding to Job's criticisms of God's providence in passages such as chapter 9 and 12:13-25. Elihu here shows no pastoral concern, he wants to beat Job into subjection. God has absolute power and is guiltless. He is in charge of everything and can do as he pleases. This is exactly what Job acknowledges in 42:2: 'I know that you can do all things; no plan of yours can be thwarted.' Elihu's words, however, contribute nothing to this change in Job, it is the vision and revelation of God himself which does this. Elihu sees God's justice as mainly punitive (verses 16ff.); a direct attack on what Job says in 9:23ff. This has none of the compassion which we have seen in Job's own speeches, notably chapter 24.

In chapter 35, Elihu turns to the subject of God's detachment - verse 5: 'Look up at the heavens and see; gaze at the clouds so high above you', and verse 6: 'If you sin, how does that affect him?' God, he alleges, does not listen to human cries because those who cry are hypocrites. Now it can be true in some cases, such as Psalm 66:18, 'If I had cherished sin in my heart, the Lord would not have listened.' But this is emphatically not the case with Job. Indeed, if Elihu is right God simply will not appear to Job, and thus it is difficult to imagine a greater marginalising of Elihu than the spectacular appearance of God which is shortly to happen. Elihu states

rightly that God is great and beyond our understanding, but reasons wrongly that because of this
he does not care for humans. The right way to
reason would have been that of Isaiah 40 where the
overwhelming grandeur of God is celebrated as a
reason for trusting him: 'Those who hope in the
LORD will renew their strength. They will soar on
wings like eagles; they will run and not grow
weary, they will walk and not be faint' (40:31).
Indeed Elihu's condemnation of Job in 35:16: 'So
Job opens his mouth with empty talk; without
knowledge he multiplies words' could be a fair
description of his own speech.

Finally in chapters 36 and 37, Elihu turns with
breathtaking self-confidence to justify the ways of
God in creation and providence. He claims a kind
of Solomonic knowledge. He argues that suffering
is sent by God to teach lessons and give people a
deeper understanding of his ways. The fundamental problem in all this is that Job has never denied
the unfathomable greatness of God; we noticed this
especially in what he says in chapter 9. Elihu
becomes eloquent as he speaks of the glories of
creation and especially the power of God in clouds,
storms and thunder. Indeed, as he speaks, a thunderstorm gathers: 'Listen! Listen to the roar of his
voice, to the rumbling that comes from his mouth'
(37:2), and it is from this storm that God speaks in
38:1. It is fascinating to see that Elihu speaks
dogmatically as if the mysteries of the universe

were an open book to him. Yet in chapter 38, in a stunning series of questions, God is to show the mystery at the heart of those things on which Elihu pronounces so confidently. Like the Friends, Elihu appears to have neither humility nor a sense of his own ignorance. He is perfectly convinced, of course, of Job's ignorance.

Elihu's final argument is a clever one from his point of view, 'No-one can look at the sun, bright as it is in the skies' (37:21). If you cannot look at the sun in its blazing splendour, how can you look on God as 'out of the north he comes in golden splendour' (37:22). Elihu is confidently stating that Job cannot expect a private appearance of God; God only answers indirectly through such means as dreams and suffering. How wrong he was! It was just such an appearance which was about to happen and to silence Elihu far more effectively than any argument.

What are we to make then of Elihu's contribution? Plainly he has said some good things and has some useful insights. Nevertheless, God does the most devastating thing possible: he simply ignores him. Nor are we shown Job's response to Elihu, for the appearance of God is so overwhelming that everything else dwindles to insignificance.

First of all there is the salutary lesson that even the speaking of truth, if it is not done from a heart of love, is more likely to lead to blindness and

confusion than to transformation. Elihu takes great
slabs of truth and constructs a monstrous edifice
without doors or windows. Worse, he uses these
same slabs as missiles to rain down on Job's head.
He knows it all and thus can learn nothing new from
the living Spirit. Thus it is that those who want to
apply the living truth to their contemporaries must
approach it in a spirit of humility and willingness to
learn themselves. Elihu's comments are not marked
by the spirit of prayer, they are the words of
someone convinced he is right and the atmosphere
is like the cold icy wind of which he speaks in
chapter 37.

The second thing is to observe that, although
Elihu probably comes nearer to the truth than the
Friends do, he does not grasp the most basic reality
about the situation: which is that Job is in no doubt
about the majesty and power of God, but has lost
confidence in God's good intentions towards him.
It is precisely in this area of relationships that the
shortcomings of all four, Elihu as well as Eliphaz,
Bildad and Zophar, are most glaring. None of them
offer to pray with Job, they are far too concerned to
convince him of the rightness of what they say.

But most important of all, Elihu is ultimately
utterly wrong because God does appear. What
follows is one of the great theophanies of Scripture:
comparable to Jacob wrestling with God (Genesis
32); Moses at the Burning Bush (Exodus 3); Isaiah
in the Temple (Isaiah 6) and John on Patmos seeing

the Risen Lord (Revelation 1). We shall examine
this in the next chapters, but it is worth noting at this
point that it is to be God himself, and not statements
about him, who is to bring the answer.

8

THE GRANDEUR OF GOD
(Job 38, 39)

In one of her famous meditations, Lady Julian of
Norwich tells of a vision in which God holds in his
hand a small round object like a nut. When Lady
Julian asked what it was, God replied 'Everything
that is'. The universe is vast, immense and mysterious, but compared with the sheer greatness of God
it is like a nut. The chapters we now consider (38
and 39) evoke both the mysteries of the universe
and the immensity of God. G. M. Hopkins speaks
of this in his poem, *The Grandeur of God,* where he
sees the living Spirit moving, penetrating, energis-
ing every living thing, but also sees the treading and
toiling generations and the dark mystery which lies
at the heart of creation. It is this mystery which we
expect God to address.

We have already looked at how the debate
appears to run into the sand after chapter 24, and
how progress appears to be further impeded by the
long speech of Elihu in chapters 33-37. Human
wisdom has been given a fair run for its money;
everyone has been allowed to speak at great length.
So when God speaks at the eleventh hour it is

significant that he speaks from a storm. In chapter 9 Job had spoken of God being active in the forces of nature at their most terrifying, in storms, earthquakes and eclipses. In chapter 1 it was a violent storm which had destroyed Job's family. Thus, right out of the heart of the mystery, God speaks.

It is also most significant that God is given his Israelite name *Yahweh*, a name which does not occur often in the book. The poet is here making the point that this is the God of the covenant, the God who is the protector of his people and who is committed to them by promises that he cannot and will not break. This is not some remote deity living far away across leagues of space. This is *Yahweh* revealing himself as the *go'el* for whom Job had longed. When he speaks out of the storm he does not give answers, he asks questions - 'Who is this that darkens my counsel with words without knowledge?'

In one sense that is putting Job in his place; there is much of which he is ignorant. In another sense it is meeting Job at his point of need and proceeding to open up dimensions of the problem of which he was totally unaware. As we explore this cascade of questions there are three areas to examine: the sheer greatness and vastness of God; the care and providence of God, and finally the joy of God.

The greatness of God

The greatness and grandeur of God shine through
every word of this majestic poem in chapters 38 and
39. For most of this book, the God perceived by the
actors in the drama has been 'too small', to borrow
the words of J. B. Phillips, the eminent Bible
translator of earlier this century. The God of the
Friends has certainly been too small, trapped in a
universe of laws of cause and effect of which he is
apparently the slave. Elihu had seen further but
lacked a becoming humility in the face of mystery.
The splendid Wisdom poem of chapter 28 had
established important truths, but these had not been
fully grasped by anyone. Job himself had seen
further and, as we have noticed, had many glimpses
of the reality and made some astonishing leaps of
faith. But no-one had seen far enough. God is far
greater, far vaster than anyone in the book has yet
realised.

Moreover, it is not just the vastness of the
universe and the miracle of its creation which is
emphasised, but God's continuing control and di-
rection of it. God is not only the Creator who, in the
beginning, created the heavens and the earth; but
the God who, day by day, continually creates and
directs: 'Have you ever given orders to the morning?' (38:12); 'Who cuts a channel for the torrents
of rain?' (38:25); 'Do you know when the mountain
goats give birth?' (39:1); 'Do you give the horse his
strength?' (39:19).

It is further noteworthy that God points out that creation does not centre around human beings. This is strikingly illustrated in 38:26: 'to water a land where no man lives, a desert with no-one in it'. Our age tends to be people and problem centred. We tend to judge people, things, situations on how they will affect us. Our theology often is made up of what will make us feel good. That tends to be where we begin and we are inclined to fashion our idea of God very subjectively. God is turning Job and turning us away from ourselves. That does not, of course, mean that we are unimportant to God and that our concerns are a matter of indifference to him. Indeed, they are so important that we must apply the right medicine, begin at the right place, and that is not ourselves. If we begin with ourselves we will simply become more and more introspective and depressed. But God is directing Job to a wider panorama and vaster horizons. It is not, however, simply vastness which God emphasises, it is the intricate and detailed network of creation. We are taken on a mind-bending tour of the cosmos, from the depths of Sheol to the great constellations in heaven, and shown wild animals in strange and exotic locations.

This leads to another aspect of the greatness of God: his awesomeness and otherness. This sense which is sometimes called the 'numinous', the feeling we have all had, perhaps on a moonlit night, by the seashore, on a woodland path or in a vast cathedral, is powerfully evoked in these chapters. This is the experience of the presence of God as a palpable reality, when the veil is thin and his presence, which is always there, becomes a felt experience. When Jacob falls asleep at the place he later calls Bethel, he has a dream of angels ascending and descending a ladder and he awakes with a sense of the awesome presence of God. John on Patmos, when he sees the Risen Christ, falls down like someone dead. A very good example, on a more popular level, is to be found in *The Wind in the Willows* when Rat and Mole approach Pan on the island:

> 'Rat,' he found breath to whisper, 'are you afraid?' 'Afraid?', murmured Rat, his eyes shining with unutterable love. 'Afraid? Of him? Oh never, never. Yet, and yet, I am afraid.'

This sheer mystery of God does far more than any refutation could to rebuke the confident platitudes of the Friends. They think they have got God taped, they think they can put him in a box. God simply sets all they have said aside, and without ever actually contradicting it, simply marginalises it. This creates the kind of atmosphere in which the further revelation of chapters 40 and 41 and the resolution of chapter 42 are possible.

The providence of God

Related to this is the second great theme of these chapters: the care and providence of God.

Essentially the theology of the Friends has seen God as a kind of heavenly policeman, an agent of law and order whose presence has proved that Job is guilty. Instead these chapters show, in Dante's words, 'the love that moves heaven, earth and all the stars'. At the heart of the universe is no remote, chilling, mechanical deity, but the loving God of Job 1.

This is brought out in the detailed way God leads Job through an exploration of the mysteries of the created world. And what a vivid and memorable journey it is: the music of the spheres, the majesty of the sea, the earth's features like clay under a seal, the swiftness of dawn, the depths of the under- world, snow, rain, hail, lightning, the procession of the seasons and the wild and strange beauty of animal life. This is not for mere poetic effect; Job's crushed and broken spirit is beginning to be healed by the beauty and mystery of the world.

Notice what God is doing: God is making Job his confidant and companion. He is saying: 'Come Job, I'm going to take you on a tour of the universe. You have seen all these things before: you have seen stars, sea and sky, you know about snow, rain, hail, eagles and horses, but you have never seen it in my company, you have never understood it from my perspective.' So God builds on Job's partial insights in earlier chapters such as 9 and 19, and by doing so leads him towards healing.

This is also strikingly developed in chapter 39. This is more than a random selection of animals chosen because God happened to like them. Rather it is a picture of the life cycle itself. 'Do you know when the mountain goats give birth?' (verse 1): this is the fundamental mystery of life, the moment of birth, to which, we may remember, Job had reacted negatively in chapter 3. Creation goes on, life is continually appearing, birth is always a reality.

Then in verses 5-12 we have two opposite examples of the fundamental mystery of the life cycle. There is, first, the mystery of freedom as the wild donkey roams the salt flats; then there is the mystery of domesticity: why is it that the wild ox cannot be pressed into service?

Then in the very centre of the chapter (verses 13-18) we have a kind of *reductio ad absurdum*, a comic vignette of the mystery of life; we laugh with the poet at the crazy antics of the ostrich: 'She lays her eggs on the ground and lets them warm in the sand, unmindful that a foot may crush them.' Yet she has a compensating swiftness which allows her to escape from predators: 'she laughs at horse and rider.'

Then we have two pictures of death, the other end of the life cycle. In verses 19-25 the warhorse, whose own wild instincts are harnessed by men in the business of war, is vividly evoked, and the

clanging consonants in the Hebrew text most effectively reinforce the vividness of the word picture.
Finally in verses 26-30 we are in the savage world
of birds of prey: 'nature red in tooth and claw', the
cruelty running through the world of nature. We
are on the verge of the sinister world of Behemoth
and Leviathan.

Now this whole chapter dramatises the mystery
of Providence and free will. These creatures are
free and untameable by humans, yet they can operate only within the limits God lays down, a point of
enormous significance for the interpretation of the
Behemoth and Leviathan passages. Moreover,
God is showing Job that this mysterious interplay
of providence and free will lies at the very heart of
creation and thus is the root of Job's problem. The
care and providence of God is not simplistic and
mechanical, it is the continuing process of his
involvement with his creation.

The joy of God
But, thirdly, there is another deep melody sounding
through these chapters, and that is the joy of God.
These chapters have the exuberance of great hymns
of praise, the note which predominates in the psalms
of praise and thanksgiving. A few examples will
illustrate this:

The heavens declare the glory of God and the
firmament shows his handiwork (Psalm 19:1).

How many are your works, O LORD! In
wisdom you made them all; the earth is full of
your creatures (Psalm 104:24).

Praise the LORD from the earth, you great sea
creatures and all ocean depths, lightning and
hail, snow and clouds, stormy winds that do
his bidding (Psalm 148:7-8).

This is especially underlined in Job 38:7:

While the morning stars sang together and all
the sons of God shouted for joy.

The whole of creation becomes a vast orchestra and
we are invited to join in the symphony of praise.

Thus the question arises: why did not Job have
an awareness of this paean of praise in chapter 3?
Why have we had to wait, as nearly forty chapters
have rolled their majestic way, to reach this point?
But Job could not simply jump from his despairing
nihilistic grief to singing and pretending everything was all right. A chorus, once popular, as-
serted that 'a little talk with Jesus makes it right, all
right'. Now the book of Job shows us how hollow
and superficial that is. We cannot simply rush from
chapter 2 to chapter 42 and pretend that the journey
of chapters 3-41 was unnecessary. If Job is going
to join in this kind of praise he has to work his way
through the darkness first. He has to go down to the

depths of Sheol before he can re-ascend to the
heavens. He has to face Leviathan and see evil
unmasked.

Two observations can be made.

The first is that God uses the same details as Job
himself had used earlier. It is no accident that he
mentions in chapter 38 exactly the same constellations as Job had mentioned in chapter 9. But the
difference is that God is revealing the secrets known
only to the Creator. The atmosphere is like that
other great chapter of creation and providence,
Isaiah 40: 'He who brings out the starry host one by
one, and calls them each by name. Because of his
great power and mighty strength, not one of them is
missing' (verse 26). Divine providence is detailed
and meticulous in its care for all it has made. It is
the fact that God is in control that matters, not what
Job or anyone else feels at a particular time. Once
again the best commentary on this is in the Psalter:

'Where can I go from your Spirit?
    Where can I flee from your presence?
If I go up to the heavens, you are there;
    if I make my bed in the depths, you are there.
If I rise on the wings of the dawn,
    if I settle on the far side of the sea,
even there your hand will guide me,
    your right hand will hold me fast'
                            (Psalm 139:7-10).

The second thing to notice is that God himself is the answer. Ultimately this is not nature poetry, but poetry about God. Healing, in other words, is not ultimately to be found in contemplation of nature. Not that there is no healing at all to be found in nature. There is a kind of healing to be found there; it is a good thing to get away from stone, lime, buildings and noise, from buses, cars and trains and go out to moorland or woodland or walk by sea or river. We all know that does us good, makes us feel better and helps us to see things in perspective.

But in situations such as those described in Job 1 and 2, nature will not heal us nor take away the aching sense of loss. We must avoid making extravagant claims for nature. Wordsworth, although a great and sensitive poet, sometimes does so, as in his unfortunate line: 'Nature never did betray the heart who loved her.' Had he never heard of tidal waves, of landslides, of earthquakes and hurricanes?

The panorama of the universe is not going to heal Job, but it is going to take him a long way to being healed. When he finally realises the truth he says, 'My ears had heard of you but now my eyes have seen you' (42:5). God does not give a slick, glib answer to the problem of evil which we can write on a postcard and produce the next time someone asks us: 'How can evil happen in a world created and governed by a good God?' What God does is give a revelation of himself. God brings Job

to the place where the real enemy can be unmasked.
Given that God is in control of the entire universe,
why is it filled with such suffering? Job is to see
God, but he is also to see the Enemy and that is the
beginning of healing and the beginning of the
answer.

9

THE ENEMY UNMASKED
(Job 40-41)

In the preface to one of his plays, Bernard Shaw speaks of Job chapters 40 and 41 and says: 'God really has to do better in explaining the problem of evil than to say "You can't make a hippopotamus can you?" ' And that nearly encapsulates the essence of the problem in these chapters. If, as many commentators argue, Behemoth is the hippopotamus and Leviathan is the crocodile, or perhaps the whale or the dolphin, then we really have to ask what all the fuss is about. Is God letting us down at the eleventh hour? Is there no further revelation in the book, no unmasking of the enemy? And why does Job react in the way he does? Why does he say in 42:5: 'My ears had heard of you but now my eyes have seen you.'

It is, of course, possible to argue that the intention of the book is to leave us in mystery and to teach us that we must trust God even in the deepest darkness. That is not an unworthy idea and, as we shall see, much mystery remains whatever view we take of the chapters. There are, however, a number of considerations which strongly suggest that this is not the main thrust of these two chapters.

The first is that God has already taught Job much in chapters 38 and 39 which we have already explored. If the Behemoth passage followed on without a break from the end of chapter 39, it would be natural to assume that it and the longer Leviathan passage were simply more of the same and were essentially reinforcing the same ideas. However, 40:1-14 contains a further dialogue between God and Job which implies that what follows is to be further revelation. Job has been filled with awe as God has conducted him through the cosmos. Yet he is puzzled, he still does not know, and we do not know, what the place and power of evil is. There has been no kind of answer as to why he is suffering. There has not yet been enlightenment about the relationship between God and evil, between God and the sinister figure whom Job believes to be attacking him.

Behemoth

Most of this chapter will be devoted to a study of Leviathan in chapter 41 but a word is needed on Behemoth (40:15-24). Behemoth is a plural form of the common Hebrew word for 'beast'. Since it is plain that a single figure is intended, it is probably an intensive plural i.e. the Beast par excellence. Some may recall William Golding's novel, *Lord of the Flies*, where a group of school boys, well brought up from public schools, are marooned on a desert island where they degenerate into appalling savages and end up destroying each other. At the centre of that novel is the sinister figure of the Beast, which is both the evil inside the boys and also comes to be identified with a pig's head on a stick in a forest glade.

Here Behemoth is an embodiment of evil and chaos. Behemoth, I suggest, is in fact the personification of death itself; death which has haunted the book and which has dominated all of Job's thoughts. Chapter 39 has ended with cruelty and death in the animal world. In 40:13 God challenges Job about the world of death:

> Bury them all in the dust together;
> shroud their faces in the grave.

This prepares us for the appearance of death itself. This is not to say that Behemoth does not have any features borrowed from the hippopotamus; this in fact serves to give him a solid reality. There are many references to myths of surrounding nations which, I have argued already, are used by the poet to illustrate profound truths about God and the world. In Egyptian legend, Seti, god of darkness, takes the form of a hippopotamus in a battle with Horus who is the god of light. In Canaanite myth the god of death lurks in marshlands very like those of verses 23,24. There is an interesting passage in Hebrews 2:14,15 where the writer says that Christ: 'shared in their humanity so that by his death he

might destroy him who holds the power of death -
that is, the devil - and free those who all their lives
were held in slavery by their fear of death.' This, I
suggest, is what these chapters are about; Behemoth is Death and Leviathan is the one who has the
power of Death, the Satan of chapters 1 and 2.

Job has been trying to understand this with
totally inadequate criteria: 'pulling out Leviathan
with a fishhook'. But at least Job has made an
attempt, which is more than his Friends have done.
There is no place in the Friends' universe for
Behemoth and Leviathan, and that is no small part
of their inadequate understanding of God. Thus we
must try to grapple with this amazing description of
Leviathan in chapter 41. Three questions demand
our attention. First of all, who is Leviathan? It has
already been suggested that Leviathan is the Satan
figure but this must now be addressed in more
detail. Secondly, in what sense is Leviathan part of
creation and under the control of God? Thirdly,
how does all this help Job and lead to the events of
Chapter 42?

Leviathan
Who is Leviathan: The starting point for tackling
this question must be the same as that for any
biblical text if we are serious about trying to understand it; that is, what would this text have meant to
those who first heard it or read it. There is no
consensus on when the book of Job was written, but

the next best thing is to study the earliest interpretations, which are much more likely to be in touch with the thinking of the original audience.

When the Jewish rabbis interpreted the book of Job, they were in no doubt at all that these creatures were the embodiment of the powers of evil, and they built up a whole elaborate mythology of the activities of these creatures from creation until the final judgment. The Greek Old Testament, the Septuagint, actually uses the word 'dragon' in place of Leviathan, thereby choosing a word with definite supernatural connotations. Indeed, nowhere, as far as I have been able to discover, do we find Behemoth and Leviathan regarded as natural creatures until the Renaissance.

In the discussion of chapters 1 and 2, I pointed out that one of the main problems in the interpretation of Job is where Satan goes after chapter 2. He apparently does not appear again and takes no further part in the action. The burden of my argument has been that he simply changes his guise. He no longer appears as the Satan, but almost immediately he features in chapter 3 in the form of Leviathan, the sea monster. And now, at the end of the poetic dialogue, we have this elaborate picture of him and so much of what has been hinted at throughout the book is about to be revealed. The Satan, master of disguise and subterfuge, disappears in his own person, but re-emerges as this figure of evil.

It is instructive first to examine the structure of the chapter. In verses 1-8 we have a series of rhetorical questions rather like those God had asked in chapters 38 and 39. This series of questions is designed to underline the gulf between Leviathan and ordinary human society, and further suggest that the problem is more than human. And many of the comments have grim irony and humour: 'Can you make a pet of him like a bird or put him on a leash for your girls?'

This section concludes with a statement which, like so many in Job, has both a surface meaning and hidden layers of meaning: 'If you lay a hand on him, you will remember the struggle and never do it again!' Many commentators see this as a description of a crocodile hunt and, as I said in the discussion of Behemoth, it is likely that natural creatures, in this case the crocodile or the whale, have been drawn on for some of the details. How else can we speak of supernatural creatures? Yet there is probably here a reference to the great battle with the forces of evil in some way associated with the creation of the world.

Verses 9-11 constitute a challenge. Leviathan is so fierce and overwhelming that even the sight of him will cause dread and dismay. How much greater then must be the power of God! These particular verses are, however, very difficult to translate and amongst the most obscure in the book.

The passage continues in verses 12-30 with a

detailed description of Leviathan. The first thing to be emphasised is the creature's armour. This emphasis is deliberate. In chapters 16 and 19 Job had accused God of attacking him like an armed warrior.

> Again and again he bursts upon me;
> he rushes at me like a warrior (16:14).

Or

> His troops advance in force; they build a
> siege ramp against me and encamp around
> my tent (19:12).

God is now unmasking the real enemy who has attacked Job like a warrior and brought his troops against him. God is, in the most effective way imaginable, helping Job to see who his titanic adversary is. The supernatural aspect of Leviathan is underlined in verses 18ff.: 'His eyes are like the rays of dawn. Firebrands stream from his mouth; sparks of fire shoot out ...'. The creature here becomes very much like the dragon of a mediaeval legend and we are far away from the world of the crocodile.

There is a deeper significance which not all commentators have grasped. We have noticed already that certain passages in Job, notably chapters 9 and 38, can be described as 'Theophany' passages: where the awesome power of God,

always present in creation, is unveiled in earthquakes, eclipses and the other massive forces of
nature. Leviathan here is exposed as imitating the
awesome presence of God which is so often symbolised by fire. In other words, God is saying to Job,
'Leviathan has masqueraded so subtly as me, that
you have actually mistaken him for me.' It is
difficult to see, even in the language of hyperbole
and exaggeration, how this can be applied to a
crocodile or a whale.

The concluding verses (31-34) of the chapter
describe the creature's haunts. His sphere is the
primaeval ocean, the *Tehom*, the abode of the
powers of chaos and darkness. Then there is the
significant reference to his lordship over the world
of the proud. All this would reinforce the awesome
impression this passage must have made on its
earliest hearers.

To round off our consideration of who Leviathan is, it is worth looking at the other places in the
Old Testament where he occurs. It is of no little
importance that he is mentioned in the Psalter. The
hymnbook of ancient Israel is the heart and essence
of its faith and shows us what was significant for
them in their worship. Psalm 74:12ff. speaks of the
power of God in creation:

> ... you broke the heads of the monster in the
> waters.
> It was you who crushed the heads of Leviathan.

This is paralleled with:

> The day is yours, and yours also the night;
>   you established the sun and the moon.

The making of heaven and earth and the curbing of the forces of darkness are mysteriously linked. The great psalm of creation, Psalm 104, speaks of the sea, vast and spacious '...and the leviathan, which you formed to frolic there' (verse 26). In face of the unapproachable transcendence of God Leviathan is cut down to size. Many other psalms such as 89 and 93 speak of God's power over the raging waters.

An interesting reference to Leviathan occurs in Isaiah 27:1:

> In that day,
>   the LORD will punish with his sword,
>   his fierce, great and powerful sword,
> Leviathan the gliding serpent,
>   Leviathan the coiling serpent;
> he will slay the monster of the sea.

'That day' is the last day, when the powers of evil will be finally crushed. This aspect is, of course, especially the concern of the book of Revelation where so many of the images and themes of the Old Testament are taken up and woven together: 'The great dragon... that ancient serpent called the devil or Satan, who leads the whole world astray' (Revelation 12:9).

All this reinforces the view that Leviathan is the Satan of chapters 1 and 2, the ancient prince of hell, the dragon, the chaos monster also called Rahab in chapters 9 and 26 and in some other places in the Old Testament.

Satan under the control of God

In what sense is Leviathan part of creation and under the control of God?

A good starting point is Isaiah 45:7: 'I form the light and create darkness, I bring prosperity and create disaster.' This is a useful reminder that in chapters 1 and 2 God not only allows, but actually incites and encourages Satan to proceed against Job.

But in what sense is God in control, and what does it mean to say that he created Behemoth and Leviathan? They are God's creatures, the powers of evil are part of creation. In Genesis 1, God creates heaven and earth which are described as 'good' or 'very good'. What place is there for the 'formlessness' and 'void' also mentioned in these chapters?

Now this is not simply an Old Testament problem; John 1:3 states: 'Through him all things were made; without him nothing was made that has been made.' And this, of course, means that death, sickness, evil and chaos must in some mysterious way be under God's control and part of God's creation.

The only viable alternative is dualism, and dualism was very popular in the Ancient Near East. Dualism essentially argues that the powers of light and darkness are equally matched and co-exist from all eternity and to all eternity. Observation of the world around us suggests that this is a very plausible view. The swing of the pendulum between good and evil in life at all levels appears to be unending.

But that view is, in every single respect, unbiblical and leaves no gospel. It is unbiblical about creation, because there is in fact no creation, simply the powers of good and evil in ceaseless and unending struggle. There is no event in the middle of history which deals the deathblow to Satan and sin. There is no final salvation because good and evil are doomed to fight for ever in sickening, see-saw equilibrium.

But there is another way to look at the evidence. The Bible, as we have seen, unequivocally states that God created everything including the Satan. Consider what God does in the act of creation: he breathes life into creatures which are other than himself, and by breathing his life into them, he gives them the capacity for choice, which includes the capacity to disobey him. Thus Satan and the powers of darkness were created by God, but not as malign creatures.

The Old Testament hints at this in picture and imagery rather than by direct statement. It speaks of a spirit, created glorious and magnificent, but who, puffed up with pride, wished to be God - the ultimate sin of a creature.

In Isaiah 14 we read of a mysterious figure, who on one level is the literal King of Babylon, who is 'brought down to the grave, to the depths of the pit' (verse 15). But the language used of this figure wishing to 'ascend to heaven', 'raise my throne above the stars of God' and 'sit enthroned on the mount of assembly' (i.e. preside at the Heavenly Court) goes far beyond any early potentate. It suggests a far more sinister power behind earthly powers, using his great intelligence to frustrate God's purposes.

Likewise in Ezekiel 26 and 28 we read of the Prince of Tyre, and this is part of Ezekiel's oracles against the various nations prominent at the time. Yet once again the language goes far beyond that of any Tyrian leader:

> You were the model of perfection,
> full of wisdom and perfect in beauty ...
> You were anointed as a guardian cherub,
>   for so I ordained you.
> You were on the holy mount of God;
>   you walked among the fiery stones.
> You were blameless in your ways
>   from the day you were created
>   till wickedness was found in you
>   (Ezekiel 28:12; 14-15).

It seems to me that what is being hinted at here is the creation of a spirit of great power, great beauty and great intelligence who falls, but retains these attributes and uses them against God and his purposes. Milton, in *Paradise Lost,* develops with great power and insight the magnificence of this figure. And that has been the thrust of my argument about Job 41, that God's enemy is still a magnificent figure.

But there is another aspect to all this. Genesis 3 speaks of another fall - the fall of human beings. Eve was tempted by the serpent, but who is the serpent? In some sense, he is simply a snake, a beast, a creature, but no Hebrew reader would fail to recognise the nuances of the word. The Hebrew word *nahash*, which is there used of the serpent, is used in Job 26:13, and in the Psalter, of Leviathan and that tells us that in Genesis 3 the power of evil is active. And it is not only humankind which is corrupted but the earth is spoiled as well and will produce thorns and thistles.

This is a theme Paul elaborates in Romans 8 when he speaks of the redemption of the whole universe: 'We know that the whole creation has been groaning as in the pains of childbirth right up to the present time ...' (Romans 8:22). Creation groans, waiting for its renewal which will follow the glorifying of the children of God. This is how creation and the place of evil belong together.

In Chapters 38 and 39 God had said to Job 'You

must look at creation the way that I look at it. You
must realise that the universe, in all its heights and
depths it is under my control. And in Chapter 40 and
41 the powers of evil, shown in astonishing detail,
are under my control as well and will ultimately
serve my good purposes.' Even Leviathan will
ultimately serve providence; the devil, as Luther
said, is God's devil.

How does this help Job?

In Chapter 42 Job finds this revelation overwhelming and describes it as the contrast between seeing
God and merely hearing about him: 'My ears had
heard of you but now my eyes have seen you'
(42:5). Two things in particular are worth noting.

First of all, Job has seen the awesome power of
evil. Never again would he be unaware of the
nature of the powers of darkness. We have already
noticed that he had glimpsed something of this
problem, notably in 9:24, 'If it is not he, then who
is it?' We have also noticed that it was ignorance of
that dimension which was one of the factors which
prevented the Friends counselling and helping Job
in his distress.

But the second and more important thing is that
Job has seen that God is in control of the powers of
evil. God knows this creature so intimately, and
describes him so powerfully, that he is showing in
the most effective possible way that he controls
Leviathan. Ultimately, the most important thing

about Satan is that Jesus Christ has defeated him. Much mystery remains; Job does not see everything. God speaks out of the tempest, veiled in mystery, but the victory has been won.

A man, walking through Berlin in the months immediately following the end of the Second World War, passed the ruins of Hitler's Chancellery, the very place where monstrous evil had been hatched. It was a beautiful day in early winter, the sun was shining and a young mother was sitting on the steps of the chancellery feeding her child. Just as the man passed, the child threw back his head and laughed and his shadow fell across the ruins of that sinister building. So it is that the shadow of another child falls across the grim empire of darkness. So it is that by the cross and resurrection Christ has broken the vicious spiral of evil and made victory possible for his followers.

10

THE VISION GLORIOUS
(Job 42)

Many people have felt a sense of anti-climax on reading Job 42. After the titanic struggles, the volcanic energy and the brilliant imagery of the previous chapters, we seem to have entered the rather smug world of an improving tale with a conventional happy ending. Worse still, is the lurking feeling that the old 'prosperity theology' has been let in the back door. To be faithful to God does really lead to material prosperity after all. Some have solved this problem by simply arguing that the chapter, especially verses 7-17, is a later addition by a pious but ungifted writer, rather like those 18th century people who gave happy endings to Shakespeare's *King Lear*.

But, as so often in *Job*, when we make hasty responses we find that the rug is pulled from under our feet and we are left gasping at the profundity and brilliance of this author, and wiser and more humble if we will only listen. Far from being an anti-climax, this chapter is a necessary concluding movement and has, as we shall see, numerous links with what has gone before. We shall look first at

Job's response to the Lord, with particular emphasis on what he means by 'seeing' God. Then we shall examine in what sense Job has 'spoken right' about God and the Friends have not. Finally we shall explore the 'happy ending' and consider whether it is a satisfactory conclusion to the book.

We have already seen how God's second speech, with its unveiling of supernatural evil embodied in Behemoth and Leviathan, brings to a climax the theology of the book. Job's response here in 42:1-6 is particularly related to that. Leviathan and his place in God's universe has been a demonstration to Job that no part of creation and no creature, however powerful, was outside the Lord's domain. The great mysteries, the farthest reaches of space and time, the thunder and lightning, the predatory beasts, the underworld itself, remained full of unsolved problems, but God had demonstrated that he was in control. Job could now look up at the night sky and into the depths of the ocean knowing that the God who made it all was good and had good purposes for him.

Job's response of humility and faith

The effect on Job of all this is demonstrated in two ways. First in verses 3 and 4 he confesses his error and acknowledges the truth of God's words. It is important to notice that he does not confess sins he did not commit, his integrity remains and God himself does not challenge this. What he does admit is ignorance and presumption. He realises that his knowledge and insight have been limited and partial, and by quoting God's very words shows he has fully accepted the revelation he has been given in chapters 38-41.

But Job goes beyond confession, and in verses 4 and 5 he expresses positively his new born faith and confidence. In particular he draws a contrast between hearing and seeing. Hearing was not to be despised; it was a necessary part of the journey, but the final goal was not to be the hearing of new insights but the vision of God himself. What does Job 'see'? This must be related to chapter 19:26, 27: 'Yet in my flesh I will see God; I myself will see him, with my own eyes.' We noticed, in our discussion of that passage, that seeing God was more important than establishing the specific time when this would happen. God, by appearing now, has vindicated Job's integrity and demonstrated that his purposes for Job are good and loving. Job had 'seen' the universe with God as his guide and that had been a revelation, not only of creation, but of the Creator.

In the creation story in Genesis 1, a major factor in the creative process is that God 'saw'. There 'seeing' is not a casual glance but an affirming that God continually looks on, cares for and provides for his creation. As in that passage, there is also the hint that one day in an unhindered way Job will see God, but that is not the main point here.

Another significant point is that this vision of God, like the vision Isaiah saw in the Temple, both fills Job with new faith and also makes him realise his unworthiness. This leads to action, symbolised by dust and ashes. We should not misunderstand the word 'repent' in verse 6. This does not mean that Job was guilty after all and is now acknowledging in effect that the Friends were right, and that he was in fact guilty of all kinds of secret sins. A more helpful comparison is with Abraham in Genesis 18:27: 'Now that I have been so bold as to speak to the Lord, though I am nothing but dust and ashes'. There Abraham is interceding for Sodom and Gomorrah, as Job is about to intercede for his Friends. Job repents, not because he has been wicked but because he has been presumptuous. Yet, like Abraham, he is a righteous man and nowhere is the righteous man more effective than on his knees.

Moreover, at the beginning of the book Job's isolation from society had been symbolised by sitting among the ashes (2:8). Now the same symbol is used for a restored relationship with God which opens the way for a restored relationship with others. It is the restoration to which we now turn.

Job's vindication and restoration

The Epilogue (42:7-17) corresponds to the Prologue (Chapters 1, 2) and reverts to narrative which completes the story. The most striking feature of

verses 7-9 is God's anger against the Friends because 'You have not spoken of me what is right as
my servant Job has'. But has not Job said some
dreadful things to God which we have already
noted on our journey through the book? We may
recall, for example, Job's bitter words such as:

> All was well with me, but he (God) shattered
> me: he seized me by the neck and crushed me
> (16:12).

> He tears me down on every side till I am
> gone; he uproots my hope like a tree (19:10).

The Friends, on the other hand, have spoken the
language of pious orthodoxy. Yet, as we noticed in
our discussion of the Friends' failure as counsellors, they imagine they can put God's case better
than he can himself. They show an unfeeling arrogance and a stupefying complacency.

In what sense has Job 'spoken what is right'
about God? In the first place he has realised that
what matters is not simply saying and knowing
correct things, but having a relationship with God.
In all his anger and confusion he has held on to this
determination to see and know God. This is an
encouragement to all who find God's ways puz-
zling and perplexing, especially if they are being
chided for their lack of faith. God is far kinder than
many of his followers, and far more ready to

welcome an honest searcher than some of his self-appointed spokesmen are.

Also, Job has shown glimpses from time to time of the supernatural origin and nature of his sufferings, for example his realisation that God may not be responsible for all the ills: 'If it is not he, then who is it?' (9:24).

It is these insights which God has built on and now put into their true perspective in chapters 38-41.

Thus the relationship is restored with God and the reconciliation with the Friends follows. Job's sacrifice and prayer is used by God in the healing and restoring of the Friends to a relationship with himself and with Job. It is further significant that three times God calls Job 'my servant'. We saw earlier how this is not simply a regular term for the faithful, but is particularly applied to figures like Moses and suggests a specially close relationship of love and obedience. Nothing could show more clearly that Job has come through to the sunshine. Not that he had ever ceased to be God's servant, but now this is being publicly acknowledged as God had initially acknowledged it to Satan himself.

God has publicly vindicated Job, he has shown that all the cruel and insensitive attacks on his honour by the Friends have been false and ill-grounded. He has shown that he does reward honest seeking and anguished protest. Just as the mysterious depths of the universe, the habits of the mountain

goat and the ostrich are in his hands so those
labyrinthine depths of human behaviour and experience are known to him and he can handle them.

But what are we to make of the 'happy ending'
(verses 7-17)? Inevitably there is a lowering of the
tension and an absence of the volcanic energy of the
earlier part of the book. After all it is cliff-hangers,
tense situations, tight corners and the like which
give excitement and suspense to a story. The writer
is now showing that Job's faith is being vindicated
in the everyday world.

Some things need to be said to put this in
context. The first is that Job wins through to a
restored relationship with God and with others
before God restores his fortunes. There is no
question of a bargain here in which Job repents
because Yahweh has blessed him. Nor is God
blessing Job as a reward for his words of contrition.
Rather, Job realises that it is God himself and not
any temporal signs of his blessing which is the real
issue. With robust faith Job had said 'The LORD
gave and the LORD has taken away; may the name
of the LORD be praised' (1:21). Now he is returning
to that faith in God himself which is ultimately not
dependent on his giving or withholding.

What is happening here is very like a pattern we
can find in many of the 'Lament' psalms where the
psalmist pours out his agony to God and then,
without any change in circumstances, triumphantly
affirms God's goodness. A good example of this is

Psalm 22 which begins with the words 'My God, my God why have you forsaken me?', but before the end there is a triumphant affirmation of faith: 'I will declare your name to my brothers; in the congregation I will praise you' (verse 22). So here, Job, without knowing that his fortunes will be restored, renews his faith and confidence in God.

The phrase in verse 10 - 'The LORD restored his fortunes again' is significant. Elsewhere it normally refers to the restoration of the nation, especially to the return of Israel from exile. The same Hebrew expression occurs in Jeremiah 29:14:

> 'I will be found by you,' declares the LORD,
> 'and will bring you back from captivity. I
> will gather you from all the nations and
> places where I have banished you,' declares
> the LORD, 'and will bring you back to this
> place from which I carried you into exile.'

Throughout the Psalms the Lord is continually praised as the Creator and the Saviour, and the saving act particularly celebrated is the Exodus. Over and over again in the Lament psalms the despair turns to hope as these great realities about God are celebrated. 'My help comes from the LORD, the Maker of heaven and earth' (Psalm 121:2), and 'When the LORD brought back the captives to Zion, we were like men who dreamed' (Psalm 126:1), are simply two examples of how the activity of God in creation and salvation is seen to have practical consequences. Something of the sort is happening here in Job 42. Job has seen the great panorama of God's power and now applies that to his own situation.

This return to normality is symbolised by a shared meal (42:11). This introduces the first note of celebration since Chapter 1. This is followed by Yahweh blessing 'the latter part of Job's life more than the first' (42:12). His family and possessions are restored abundantly and his life stretches out to the kind of length associated with the days of the patriarchs.

What is important to notice here is that the security Job now enjoys is in God himself. There is no more security in the new family and possessions than the old one. In other words there is still need for faith and the vision of God. The point is that the faith Job now has is incalculably deeper and more mature than it was in Chapter 1. Job's life still has many years to run, one hundred and forty, in fact, and no guarantee is given that these years will be trouble free.

Three things can be said to sum up the chapter. The first is that earthly blessing and prosperity are important, particularly in the Old Testament world where the full light of the Resurrection was not yet known. All that God gives here: family, wealth and renewed prosperity, are good in themselves and, while not rewards for good conduct, are gifts of

God's grace. These are the very blessings for which
we regularly pray and which form a large part of our
lives.

Secondly, this chapter emphasises the importance of right relationships. Ultimately what matters
is knowing God, and that leads to the healing of
relationships with others. Suffering has refined Job
and released hidden depths in him, yet his intercession for the Friends at the end is of a piece with his
intercession for his family at the beginning. Job had
earlier said: 'But he knows the way that I take;
when he has tested me, I shall come forth as gold'
(23:10). All the way Job has longed for and fought
for a new understanding and close relationship with
God and this is what he has now been given.

And the third thing is the emphasis on God's
creating power and his renewing love. All through
the book of Job the question of God the Creator and
his purposes has been at the very heart of the debate.
Job has never doubted the awesome power of God,
what he often had doubted was that his purposes
were loving. Chapter 42 illustrates and emphasises
God's love in the most striking way. The emphasis
on 'blessing' and 'restoring fortunes' is one of the
most striking features of the chapter and these
words are full of the sense of God's creating and
sustaining power. The numbers of livestock reinforce the sense of vibrant and abundant life that
reminds us of the creation story in Genesis 1.
Similarly the beauty of Job's daughters remind us

of how God looked on creation and pronounced it good.

So the book ends with the death of Job at a ripe old age surrounded by his family. We cannot, however, quite leave it there and in our final chapter we shall take the story on in to the New Testament.

11

JOB REVISITED

Many years ago, Dr. G. Campbell Morgan, Minister of Westminster Chapel, London wrote a book called *The Answers of Jesus to Job*. He took many of the cries of Job and showed that the only answer to these is to be found in Jesus himself.

The purpose of this present book has been rather different; it has been to take the book of Job on its own terms, and while frequent reference has been made to the New Testament, my main concern has been to expound the message of Job as it stands. However, it would be helpful to say something of the place of the book, not just in the Old Testament but in the canon of Scripture as a whole.

A Christian reading Job sees it in the light of the Cross and the Empty Tomb. It is also important to see it in the light of Jesus' teaching about the Kingdom of God and the radical and uncomfortable question marks this places against many of our assumptions.

To make this a manageable topic I thought it would be useful to concentrate on the Gospel of Mark. I choose this for two reasons.

First, in Mark the gospel is expressed in its

briefest and most concentrated form and the issues raised most starkly.

Secondly, the particular emphasis of Mark is on Jesus as the Suffering Servant. Few Old Testament passages are closer in spirit to Job than Isaiah 53 with its moving and profound picture of the Servant who is the Sufferer.

What I want to do is to look at some of the main aspects of Mark's teaching about Jesus and say something of how they throw light on the questions the Job poet grapples with. This will help us to reflect further on many of the issues and problems raised by the Old Testament book.

Five main issues will be explored: Jesus' preaching of the Kingdom; the activities of Satan; Jesus' miracles; his passion and his resurrection.

Jesus' preaching of the Kingdom

The term 'Kingdom of God', while rooted in the Old Testament is not used in Job itself; yet the issues raised by it are close to the heart of what Job is about. The life Job lives in chapter 1 (more fully described in chapter 29) is an example of the kind of lifestyle of someone who is expressing the rule of God in his life. It is a life marked by righteousness and justice and the smile of God's blessing. But there are deeper connections as well. The kingdom comes by suffering and apparent disaster; it has already come in Jesus but not fully until he returns in glory.

Moreover, Jesus in Mark, like Job is popular and
admired at the beginning. This is seen in such
statements as: 'Everyone is looking for you' (1:37);
'the people still came to him from everywhere'
(1:45); 'a large crowd came to him' (2:13); 'Jesus
entered a house and again a crowd gathered'(3:20);
'the crowd that gathered round him was so large
that he got into a boat'(4:1). However, a startling
reversal has taken place by the Passion narratives.
As we shall see, Mark particularly emphasises the
utter loneliness and isolation of Jesus.

It is not difficult to see parallels to this in the
experience of Job as a glance at chapters 29 and 30
will demonstrate. Chapter 29 gives a glowing picture of Job's life: 'When God watched over me,
when his lamp shone upon my head' (29:2, 3).
Indeed this whole chapter is an illustration of the
life of God's Kingdom in action. Job rescues the
poor and fatherless (verse 12); he 'was eyes to the
blind and feet to the lame' (verse 15); he speaks
with authority: 'Men listened to me expectantly,
waiting in silence for my counsel' (verse 21), just as
Jesus spoke with authority (Mark 1:27). Yet by
chapter 30 terror and isolation have replaced peace
and community: 'Surely no-one lays a hand on a
broken man when he cries for help in his distress.'

Two observations follow from this. The first is
that in the Kingdom of God suffering and isolation
are inevitable. The friends of Job did not grasp this
and advocated a simplistic link between goodness

and prosperity. The growing hostility to Jesus shows that far from disaster being a sign of God's displeasure, it is rather an inevitable part of the coming of the kingdom: 'For whoever wants to save his life will lose it, but whoever loses his life for me and for the gospel will save it' (Mark 8:35). Job, in fact, in his innocent suffering and the misrepresentation to which he is subjected is a very clear picture of Christ himself.

The other observation is that the suffering must be seen in the wider perspectives of the purposes of God. Mark 8:38 speaks of the Son of Man coming 'in his Father's glory'. Thus the hardship is placed in a much wider context as God puts Job's suffering in such a context in chapters 38-41. So we find that both Testaments speak with a common voice on how glory and suffering belong together.

Activities of Satan

But Mark, like Job, sees far deeper causes behind suffering than simple misfortune. We come to the second area of consideration which is the role of Satan who appears early in Mark as he does in Job. Moreover, once again Satan's initiative is intertwined with that of God: 'At once the Spirit drove him into the desert, and he was in the desert for forty days being tempted by Satan' (Mark 1:12, 13).

The New Testament elsewhere draws an important connection between the coming of the kingdom and the defeat of Satan: 'The reason the Son of God appeared was to destroy the devil's work' (1 John 3:8). This both underlines the reality of the demonic and the necessity of God's own intervention in dealing with it. This intervention of Satan at the beginning of Jesus' ministry is like that at the beginning of Job, it is an attempt to deflect God's servant (a word used of Job as well as Jesus) from his appointed path.

As in Job the assaults of Satan continue in a deeper way. There is the interesting passage in Mark 3:20-30 where 'The teachers of the law who came down from Jerusalem said, "He is possessed by Beelzebub! By the prince of demons he is driving out demons".' This is a fascinating parallel with many passages we have already noticed in Job where his Friends accuse him of belonging to that sinister underworld (notice especially Bildad's speech about the 'King of Terrors' in chapter 18).

But most striking is the reference in the Gethsemane narrative: 'He took Peter, James and John along with him, and he began to be deeply distressed and troubled. "My soul is overwhelmed with sorrow to the point of death" ' (Mark 14:33, 34).

The words translated 'deeply distressed' and 'troubled' are very strong indeed and suggest a kind of shrinking horror and dismay. Moreover, there is the suggestion of powerful, unseen, supernatural presences, of death and Satan pressing in on Jesus as the devil returns to avenge the defeats suffered in

the wilderness, the lake of Galilee and numerous
other places.

What these passages indicate is that attack by
Satan is inescapable in the endeavour to serve God.
The inadequacy of Job's Friends' explanations of
his calamities is even more starkly underlined.
Jesus himself met such conflict and was subjected
to similar misrepresentation. It is necessary, therefore, to realise and account for the presence of the
demonic. Failure to do this led Job's Friends to
regard him as suffering punishment for evil and Job
himself to misunderstand God's purposes.

The miracles of Jesus

The whole theme of the supernatural continues in
the Marcan accounts of Jesus' miracles. To make
this third area manageable I shall concentrate on
two miracles: Jesus' calming the storm (Mark 4:35-
41), and the healing of a demon-possessed man
(Mark 5:1-20), which also are closely related to one
of the central concerns in Job.

In much of Job, as we have seen, the untamed sea
is a symbol of the powers of chaos and evil which
only God can control. In Mark (and in the corre-
sponding passages in Matthew 8:23-27 and Luke
8:22-25) Jesus' rebuke of the sea is followed by the
casting out of the demons from the unfortunate man
and the precipitate descent of the swine into the sea.
These two stories plainly belong together and underline the connection made in Job and elsewhere

in the Old Testament between the evil spirits and the sea.

One or two points are worth noting. The first is that the verb Jesus uses of rebuking the sea in 4:38 (*epitimesen*) is used of rebuking an evil spirit in 1:25, as well as being followed by the story of the Gerasene demoniac. Thus it is plain that Jesus is commanding an evil power to be silent. This is confirmed by the use of the other verb in verse 39 - 'be still' (*pephimoso*), also used in 1:25. Jesus is here carrying the power of the Kingdom of God into the kingdom of darkness.

This explains the awestruck question of the disciples in verse 41: 'who then, is this, that even the winds and the sea obey him'. Now this story comes at a series of 'mighty acts': exorcism, healing, unprecedented authority in preaching. All of these, of course, have many Old Testament parallels: e.g. Saul's evil spirit removed by David's playing; healings and even raising the dead by Elijah and Elisha; the inspired utterances of the prophets. Thus there was inevitable controversy (most of it reflected within the disciples themselves) about who Jesus of Nazareth was. Most of his mighty acts were not unique - others had done so much - but surely there was only one who could say to the proud waves, 'Thus far you shall come and no further'?

Central to the miracles of Jesus is his authority over the whole of creation and the 'principalities and powers'. We have already seen in our study of Job's life that he had become the battleground of spiritual powers, and that we were dealing not merely with misfortune but with the deepest issues of creation, evil and the mysteries of life and death. Solely in Jesus, who not only suffers the same kind of agonies as Job, but also brings life out of them, can we truly find answers to the huge problems raised by the Old Testament book.

The death of Jesus

And that brings us to our fourth area which is the passion and death of our Lord. In Mark the isolation and anguish of Jesus is powerfully conveyed.

In the Gethsemane narrative, already mentioned, Mark underlines Jesus' complete loneliness. In Luke's account of the event: 'An angel from heaven appeared to him and strengthened him' (Luke 22:42).

In Mark, the identity of Peter, James and John and his desire for their companionship is emphasised, and the consequent desolation of Jesus as they fail to watch with him. This is compounded by their flight - 'everyone deserted him and fled' - and the denial of Peter, aggravated in Mark by his cursing and swearing (14:71).

In Luke 23:26-31 women follow and sympathise with Jesus, in Mark they 'were watching from a distance' (Mark 15:40). Jesus' last recorded words in the Passion Narrative in Mark are 'My God, my God why have you forsaken me?'

When we compare this with the experience of Job we find many parallels. A particularly powerful passage is Job 19:13ff.:

He has alienated my brothers from me;
  my acquaintances are completely estranged
                               from me.
My kinsmen have gone away,
  My friends have forgotten me.

In that passage, the terrible isolation that Job feels is compounded by the awful feeling that it is God himself who has brought this isolation on him. Similarly, in 30:10 Job speaks of the hatred and contempt of those who had once respected him:

They detest me and keep their distance,
  they do not hesitate to spit in my face.

To isolation had been added ridicule and mockery, the same grim details as we have in the passion narrative in Mark 15:65.

These comparisons are obvious enough and illustrate again the way in which Jesus totally identified himself with suffering humanity. If that were all, however, the depiction of suffering both in Job and Mark would remain a powerful statement of human agony and distress, but not in itself point to any answers.

Two important details, however, in Mark's account point forward and recall similar emphasis in Job. The first is the tearing of the curtain of the temple from top to bottom (15:38) symbolising that now there is free access to the presence of God. Because Jesus' suffering gathers into it all the sin and suffering of the ages, others can now approach God through his sacrifice. Job's longing for a mediator and for access to the heavenly court thus finds its answer.

The other is the words of the centurion: 'Surely this man was the Son of God' (15:39). This is a moment of revelation comparable to 'My ears had heard of you, but now my eyes have seen you' (Job 42:5). In both cases, insight and vision follows suffering and tragedy.

The resurrection of Jesus

One more topic remains. We have already noted, especially in the discussion of Job 19, how Job had glimpses of something, or rather someone, beyond death itself who would put everything right in the heavenly court. Not until the Resurrection of Jesus, however, could that hope be clearly focused and realised. We have looked, in the context of the book itself, at Job's great leap of faith in 19:25:

I know that my Redeemer lives,
and that in the end he will stand upon the earth...

Without the Resurrection these words remain ultimately a pious wish. Only the words of Mark

16:6 give them content: 'He has risen! He is not here. See the place where they laid him.' It is this event which makes sense of all the unsatisfied longings and cries of agony from Job and others.

There is one specific part of Mark's Resurrection account which is particularly relevant to Job. Nearly all scholars agree that Mark originally ended his Gospel at 16:8: 'Trembling and bewildered, the women went out and fled from the tomb. They said nothing to anyone, because they were afraid.'

This very vividly reminds us that this event was beyond human understanding and thus caused fear and trembling. Mark has frequently underlined the confusion and fear that people have felt as they have not been able to understand who Jesus is. To put it another way: the fact that Christ is risen still requires the response of faith and humility. Similarly, we noticed that at the end of the book, Job still needs to trust in God.

I think what has been said shows that we can trace many echoes of Job's suffering, as well as the answer to his cries in the life, death and resurrection of Jesus.

One or two observations will be helpful in summing up. It is plain that suffering is an integral part of what it means to be God's servant. Job is described as 'my servant', Jesus is presented as Isaiah's 'Suffering Servant', and in both cases Satan attacks and the whole basis of their dependence on God is questioned. To be a servant is to run

the risk of encountering a hostile and dangerous
world where all the familiar certainties will dissolve. This will not mean that the servant has been
unfaithful; in some mysterious way faithfulness is
tested and strengthened by adversity: 'when he has
tested me, I shall come forth as gold' (Job 23:10).

A related theme is that Jesus is not only another
servant of God, but the Servant who is God himself
and whose self-giving not only exemplifies but
heals the sufferings of his other servants. We looked
earlier at Job's cries for an advocate in the heavenly
court, culminating in chapter 19. In Jesus, that
advocate, who is also the suffering servant, is
found.

As we have seen, much of the book of Job is
magnificent poetry and it is with poetry I want to
end: George Herbert, in his poem *The Collar* chafes
under God's discipline, but through the suffering
eventually hears and welcomes a well-loved voice:

I struck the board, and cried, 'No more,
        I will abroad' ...
But as I raved and grew more fierce and wild
        At every word,
Me thought I heard one calling, 'Child'.
        And I replied 'My Lord'.

Further Reading

COMMENTARIES:

a. Large Scale:
E. Dhorme: *A Commentary on the Book of Job* (Trans. by H Knight, Nelson, 1967). First published in 1926! Still indispensable. Introduction is magnificent.

R Gordis: *The Book of Job: Commentary, New Translation and Special Notes* (New York, 1978) - Humane and penetrating Jewish scholarship.

D.J.A. Clines: *Job (1-20)*: (Word 1989): massive, learned and penetrating (Vol. II to come).

b. Medium Size:
J.E. Hartley: *The Book of Job* (N.I.C.O.T., 1986): Clear and readable, enormously useful footnotes.

N.C. Habel: *The Book of Job: A Commentary* (O.T.L., 1985): Well-written; sees text as whole and marvellous on literary aspects; I recommend this as best current substantial commentary.

M.H. Pope: *Job Introduction, Translation and Notes* (Anchor, 1973): Very useful on mythological background.

H.H. Rowley: *The Book of Job* (N.C.B., 1970): Very useful on opinion to that time, now largely superseded.

c. Smaller

F.I. Andersen: *Job: An Introduction and Commentary* (Tyndale, 1976): well-argued and detailed.

J.C.L. Gibson: *Job* (D.S.B., 1985): fine, hard-hitting theological study; another good 'buy'.

D. Atkinson: *Job* (Bible Speaks Today, IVP 1992): Good on pastoral issues.

STUDIES

Specifically on Job

J.H. Eaton: *Job* (Old Testament Guide - Sheffield, 1985) - useful survey of major issues.

R.B. Zuck (Ed.): *Sitting with Job: Selected Studies on the Book of Job* (Baker, 1992) - many useful extracts from major commentaries - good way into these.

L. Perdue and W.C. Gilpin (Ed.): *The Voice from the Whirlwind: Interpreting the Book of Job* (Abingdon, 1992) - fascinating essays on theological issues.

R. Gordis: *The Book of God and Man: A Study of Job* (Chicago, 1965) - profound reflections by a distinguished Jewish scholar.

Related Areas:

M.K. Wakeman: *God's Battle with the Monster: A Study in Biblical Imagery* (Leiden, 1973) - good thorough study of the theme.

J. Day: *God's Conflict with the Dragon and the Sea: Echoes of a Canaanite myth in the Old Testament* - thorough and detailed; rather lacks literary sense.

J.C.L. Gibson: *Canaanite Myths and Legends* (Edinburgh, 1977) - indispensable for Canaanite background.

N.J. Tromp: *Primitive Conceptions of Death and the Nether World in the Old Testament* (Rome, 1969) - useful survey of O.T. concepts of death and Sheol.

The above is a sample; the literature is vast and increasing. The main thing is to become thoroughly familiar with the text of Job. Read various translations (RSV and NIV both effective) including those in the commentaries.

Other books dealing with Old Testament subjects
published by Christian Focus Publications

Jesus, Divine Messiah -
The Old Testament Witness
Robert Reymond

The author, Professor of Systematic Theology
at Knox Theological Seminary, Florida, USA,
takes eight descriptions of the Messiah found in
the Old Testament and shows how Jesus fulfilled
each one.

ISBN 0 906 731 941   *128 pages*   large format

Songs of Experience
Roy Clements

The author is pastor of Eden Baptist Church,
Cambridge, England. In this book he explains
the relevance for today of selected psalms which
deal with living for God.

ISBN 1 85792 019 8   *208 pages*   B format

Freedom Through Obedience
George Philip

In this book the Ten Commandments are explained and applied. The author is a pastor of
the Church of Scotland in Glasgow

ISBN 0 906 731 909   *192 pages*   A format

Focus on the Bible Commentary series

Jonah, Micah and Nahum
John L Mackay
ISBN 1 85792 03 09   *240 pages*   B format

Haggai, Zechariah and Malachi
John L Mackay
ISBN 1 85792 06 78   *350 pages*   B format

Both commentaries are written by the Professor of Old Testament in the Free Church College, Edinburgh, Scotland. They are useful for both pastors and Bible Study leaders as well as helping individuals understand the teachings of these Old Testament prophets.

The series covers both Old and New Testaments. Other volumes currently available include:

Mark by *Geoffrey Grogan*
Romans by *R C Sproul*
Ephesians by *R C Sproul*
Philippians by *Hywel Jones*
James by *Derek Prime*

Other titles are currently in preparation and will be published in due course.

The authors come from different countries, but each is committed to an evangelical understanding of Scripture.

Dr. Robert Fyall is Old Testament tutor at St John's College, Durham, England. He is a graduate of the universities of St Andrews, Dundee and Edinburgh. In addition to his college duties, he is committed to a preaching and teaching ministry, being especially involved in Christian unions.